W9-BCN-227

Designed by Gillian Greenwood

Roger Manvell

New
cinema
in the USA

The feature film since 1946

studio vista|dutton pictureback
general editor David Herbert

Acknowledgements

I would like first of all to acknowledge the invaluable help I have received from **Robin Bean** in the selection of stills for this volume.

My thanks are also due to the following distributors: Academy Cinemas, Allied Artists, America International Pictures, British Lion, Columbia, Eros Films, Lopert Films, Metro-Goldwyn-Mayer, Paramount, the Rank Organisation, R.K.O. Radio, Republic, Twentieth Century-Fox, United Artists, Universal-International, Warner-Pathé, Warner Brothers. I would also like to thank John Gillett and the staff of the Stills Section of the National Film Archive at the British Film Institute for their help and information.   R. M.

© Roger Manvell 1968
Published in London by Studio Vista Limited
Blue Star House, Highgate Hill, N 19
and in New York by E. P. Dutton and Co Inc
201 Park Avenue South, New York 3, NY
Distributed in Canada by General Publishing Co Ltd
30 Lesmill Road, Don Mills, Ontario
Set in 8D on 9 pt Univers, 2 pts leaded
Made and printed in Great Britain by
Richard Clay (The Chaucer Press), Ltd, Bungay, Suffolk

SBN 289 37038 8 (paperback)
SBN 289 37039 6 (hardback)

Contents

American cinema: world cinema

American films have inevitably excited strong reactions in Europe ever since the first period of their ascendency in the cinemas over fifty years ago. If we accept that the screens (cinema and television) have combined to become the most powerful medium for popular culture in the twentieth century, then the predominant place occupied by American films in most European cinemas, at least since 1920, represents a form of cultural landslide in favour of the United States. The quota barriers gradually erected by various governments to protect their indigenous film industries have only partially affected this situation.

The Miracle Worker 1960. Director Arthur Penn
Anne Bancroft and Patty Duke

The influence of American culture in Europe was negligible before the cinema came to give it a great commercial outlet. Since the war television has made the small screen's representation of the American way of life an almost daily experience for most Europeans and, indeed, for people in many other parts of the world. For most countries in Europe except Britain, the barrier of language has acted as a partial, but only a partial, restraint. In the case of Britain, the almost common language of the two countries seemed to place no real barrier between the complete absorption by the American producers of the less powerful British film industry. The first Quota Act of 1928 made an initial ratio of British to American films which exhibitors were obliged to show a mere 1 : 20. The effective ratio over the years has been approximately two-thirds American to one-third British films in British cinemas. But by undertaking the production of British films themselves, American producers have been able to share in British quota production. It was well known that by the second half of the 1960s some three-quarters of the principal British feature films produced had in fact become either wholly or partially American-sponsored.

The United States has had inevitably to reckon with varying measures of resistance to her economic and cultural invasion of the European screen in general, and to the British screen in particular. These resistances, which have haunted internal relations within the British and American film industries for half a century, are scarcely known to the general public. They are aware only of certain obvious points about American films. First of all, they know well by long experience that American producers are prepared to spend money lavishly in order to excite wonder and admiration for the images they achieve on the screen—lavish sets, lavish locations, lavish action are the rule, not the exception, in American-sponsored films. Secondly, they know that, by and large, American films are produced to entertain by people who have made it their profession to understand entertainment, and who also know how to persuade audiences that they are in fact being entertained—that they are by their very presence in the cinema playing an active part in shaping current fashions of entertainment. Thirdly, they know that America's pursuit of the right star for the right star vehicle is a very assured business and that, by and large, no one gets into the top bracket who has not climbed there in the face of the fiercest competition for survival. So, public thinking goes, the stars in American films simply have to be accepted as good and likeable, whether in fact you like them individually or not. So success breeds taste, and what we call 'culture'. American films represent therefore a form of international culture which is as unique as it is successful.

The American producers normally pass their product through an exacting process devised to ensure its success in advance of release. At one stage, American films were hall-marked by their studios and subject to mass-production methods. More recently, standards of entertainment have been re-set by the higher-ranking American 'independent' producers in their determination to re-capture audiences lost to television. They have managed to free themselves from certain of the restraints originally imposed during the 1930s by the American censorship code. American film-making, at its best, has never been higher in standard than during the 1950s and 1960s; the better films have become more varied, more individual and enterprising, and more striking in their technical presentation than they have ever been in the past. The stereotypes of entertainment still exist, but they are less obtrusive. Individuality of talent has been found to pay, and accorded a place in the new spectrum of success.

The following brief account of the post-war American feature film attempts to show how these changes have come about during the span of some twenty-five years, and to give credit to those film-makers primarily responsible. In spite of the apparent avidity in America for anything new, it is very difficult to change basic American public taste. The 'new waves', the avant-garde, are strictly for the cults; they are activities which occur outside the mainstream of cinema, even though, now and then, some 'fringe' idea is borrowed and popularised to add a kick to convention. The great American film-makers, therefore, can only overcome old conventions by imposing new ones more to their taste, taking their world public along with them by the hundred million—a far more difficult feat than the old sport of 'shocking the bourgeois' or exciting cliques which in any case live on over-excitement.

The main 'types' of American films must be considered at the same time as we discuss how the more creative American film-makers have managed to beat these types at their own game and emerge with something at the same time individual and admirable. Perhaps it is just this quality which makes American cinema so rewarding to study.

New realism 1946

It is, of course, quite wrong to accept that there was no 'realism' in American films until the war blasted the artificial cobwebs out from the Hollywood 'dream factory'. After all, the 1920s had produced *Greed* (which its director Stroheim, claimed to be 'neo-realist') over twenty years before Rossellini made *Rome, Open City*, Sternberg's *The Docks of New York* and Vidor's *The Crowd*, and the 1930s such films as *The Story of Louis Pasteur* (Dieterle), *Fury* (Lang), *I am a Fugitive from a Chain Gang* (Leroy), *Of Mice and Men* (Milestone) and *Dead End* (Wyler). The coming of sound in itself undoubtedly drew all films closer to actuality, however hard both stars and stories clung to the older fantasies. But if by realism we mean that the kind of people we meet on the screen are of the same species we meet in real life, and the kind of problems in which they are involved (however extreme) are recognisably problems which ordinary people might have to face, then the American cinema of the 1930s provided few enough examples of realistic films.

The war, like any social catastrophe, induced a more serious attitude in the majority of people, to themselves and to their

The Best Years of Our Lives 1946. Director William Wyler
Hoagy Carmichael, Harold Russell, Fredric March

Call Northside 777 1947. Director Henry Hathaway
James Stewart

Opposite: **The Naked City** 1948. Director Jules Dassin
Unit on Location

relationship with others. Audiences were prepared to support films which attempted to face up to certain realities of war, and in consequence expected the characters in these films to bear some resemblance to themselves and to behave in a credible manner. The period 1939 to 1946 (with the United States herself entering the war after Pearl Harbor in December 1941) saw not only war films such as Lewis Milestone's *A Walk in the Sun* and William Wellman's *The Story of G.I. Joe,* but films which gave reality to other aspects of American life, such as *The Grapes of Wrath* (John Ford), *The Southerner* (Jean Renoir), *The Lost Weekend* (Billy Wilder) and Orson Welles's *Citizen Kane,* a film introducing techniques which went beyond mere surface realism into extreme forms of stylisation. One of the finest of the realistic studies of American society to appear immediately post-war was Wyler's *The Best Years of Our Lives,* produced by Sam Goldwyn in 1946. In this the various problems facing a group of men returned from the war was treated in some depth, seriously and sympathetically. Not all of these films enjoyed a conventional box-office success, though some, such as *The Best Years of Our Lives,* certainly did.

What really introduced a documentary style of realism into the American cinema in the form of a small but distinct 'movement' was the group of post-war crime films shot mainly on location in the open streets of busy cities. They followed one another in quick succession: *The House on 92nd St* (Henry Hathaway, 1945), *13 Rue Madeleine* (Hathaway, 1946), *Call Northside 777*

Act of Violence 1948. Director Fred Zinnemann
Van Heflin

and *Kiss of Death* (Hathaway, 1947), *Boomerang* (Elia Kazan, 1947), *The Naked City* (Jules Dassin, 1948), *The Window* (Ted Tetzlaff, 1948), *Act of Violence* (Fred Zinnemann, 1948), *The Street with no Name* (William Keighley, 1948), *They Live by Night* (Nicholas Ray, 1949), *The Set-up* (Robert Wise, 1949) and *Panic in the Streets* (Kazan, 1950). The characteristics of these films—their drama acted out in surroundings which were either real or bore every impression of reality, their actors for the most part giving performances from which all actorish mannerisms were removed, a candid-camera style of photographic coverage giving a new flexibility to the treatment of action, and an authentic revelation of certain processes and techniques in crime detection stemming from wartime documentary and the pre-war *March of Time* magazine series—combined actuality with entertainment and gave screen fiction a new kind of verisimilitude which was to be developed later to great advantage in more ambitious productions than these initial, mostly low-budget pictures. The initiator was Louis de Rochemont, formerly producer of the *March of Time*, and sponsor of the first films directed by Hathaway; he claimed on the screen that 'all the events depicted . . . were photographed, wherever possible, in the actual locale'; and some of the films presented true stories, and even introduced as non-professional actors people who had been associated with the original events shown. *The House on 92nd St* even introduced FBI film material of Nazi agents in action. Elia Kazan's early film, *Boomerang* (with Dana Andrews), was based on a true story and set in a town in New England. An innocent man is framed for murder owing to political pressures at the time of a local election. In spite of threats which might at the very least break him and his family, the local District Attorney secures an acquittal. Kazan followed this success with *Panic in the Streets* (with Richard Widmark), an exciting melodrama concerning the hectic search for the infected murderer of a man who is discovered to have had bubonic plague.

Panic in the Streets 1950. Director Elia Kazan

This, too, was characteristically shot entirely on location. The year before Robert Wise had made *The Set-up* (with Robert Ryan) which pulled no punches in exposing the savagery with which corruption affects a sport such as commercial boxing. Films dealing with crime, delinquency and life in jail were to develop with increasing violence in later years—films of which Don Siegel's *Riot in Cell Block 11* (1954) is typical. Other films which sometimes adopted realist techniques to give actuality to fantasy were the science-fiction films such as Robert Wise's *The Day the Earth Stood Still* (1951) and George Pal's *The War of the Worlds* (1953).

The Set-up 1949. Director Robert Wise
Robert Ryan

Riot in Cell Block 11 1954. Director Don Siege

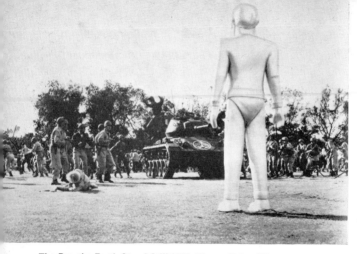

The Day the Earth Stood Still 1951. Director Robert Wise

These films were followed by others dealing specifically with social and psychological problems in which the American cinema made an ambitious attempt to combine entertainment with varying degrees of 'significance'. During the five years immediately after the war, the following films appeared: *Gentleman's Agreement* (Kazan, 1947), *Crossfire* (Edward Dmytryk, 1947, adapted from Richard Brook's first novel), *The Snake Pit* (Anatole Litvak, 1948), *The Quiet One* (Sidney Meyers, 1948), *Intruder in the Dust* (Clarence Brown, 1949), *Pinky* (Kazan, 1949), *All the King's Men* (Robert Rossen, 1949), *The Dividing Line* (Joseph Losey, 1949), *The Men* (Zinnemann, 1950) and *Fourteen Hours* (Hathaway, 1951).

These films dealt with psychological disturbance (*The Snake Pit, The Quiet One, Fourteen Hours*), rehabilitation of servicemen (*The Men*), race prejudice (*Crossfire, The Dividing Line, Gentleman's Agreement, Pinky, Intruder in the Dust*). American films often over-state their case, break down into emotionalism or indulge in sensation; it is as if these are the only means open to film-makers to hold audiences conditioned into apathy by the daily assault of the press, radio and fiction on their unsteady nerves. Sensationalising was the obvious fault of *The Snake Pit*, which met with trouble from the British censorship as a result not of its subject but the treatment it had been given. *The Snake Pit* (with Olivia de Havilland and Leo Genn) showed how a mentally disturbed woman confined in a state mental institution dehumanised

16

by regulations is cruelly misused by the staff and how, in consequence, her condition worsens until she is, in effect, rescued by a sympathetic psychiatrist. Kazan's early film, *Gentleman's Agreement* (with Gregory Peck), suffered similarly from over-dramatisation; it showed what happens to a non-Jewish journalist who poses as a Jew in order to experience race prejudice at first hand. In his previous film, *Pinky*, Jeanne Crain plays a girl who, although in fact coloured, passes for white. In this quiet and sympathetic film no easy solution to racial tensions in the United States was offered or implied. Yet it was *Gentleman's Agreement* which won the Oscars.

Crossfire 1947. Director Edward Dmytryk
Robert Ryan

Not that dramatisation is in itself wrong. *Fourteen Hours* (with Richard Basehart) made skilful, legitimate and sympathetic use of tension in the case of a young man who has worked himself on to the ledge of a tall building high above the city street and is only saved from suicide by the patient understanding of a police officer (played by Paul Douglas). The film, directed by Henry Hathaway on a six-week schedule, remains one of his best productions; ingenious use was made of camera-angle to intensify the situation of the man confined on a narrow ledge for the full length of the picture.

Fourteen Hours 1951. Director Henry Hathaway
Richard Basehart

The Quiet One 1948. Director Sidney Meyers

Both *The Quiet One* and *Intruder in the Dust* remain outstanding films in their period by virtue of their subtlety. The problems posed are never sensationalised, nor is the audience importuned. In *The Quiet One* a lonely Negro boy, wholly withdrawn, is gradually brought back by understanding treatment into association with

19

his fellows; in *Intruder in the Dust* an elderly Negro is wrongly accused of shooting a white man. As he awaits trial, the prejudices in the small southern town which is the setting for the story reach a degree of tension which could lead to a lynching. The old man, frightened yet dignified, is no more an idealised character than de Sica's Umberto D, nor are the small group of white men led by a lawyer determined to defend him, themselves wholly free from race prejudice. ('He wasn't in trouble. *We* were in trouble,' says the lawyer.) A further perspective was added in the guarded

Intruder in the Dust 1949. Director Clarence Brown
Juano Hernandez

friendship which develops between the Negro, played by Juano Hernandez, and Chick, the lawyer's callow, 16-year-old nephew. Joseph Losey's *The Dividing Line* exposed both class and racial intolerance in the Californian town of Santa Marta, while in Dmytryk's *Crossfire* racial intolerance is explored in reverse, from the side of those guilty of it. A Jew is found murdered, and the action concerns the emergence of the guilty man from among three soldiers who are suspect. The film makes an unsentimental plea for tolerance.

The Dividing Line 1949. Director Joseph Losey

One of the strongest films made during this post-war period was *All the King's Men* (with Broderick Crawford and Mercedes McCambridge). It was produced, scripted and directed by Robert Rossen, and was conceived on a larger scale than most of the social films of the period. It showed how a corrupt, small-town political operator called Willie Stark develops his power to the point when he becomes a menace to a whole region in the State. The film has a striking air of authenticity in its treatment; it develops leisurely, with more concern for character and detail than a tight dramatic structure. In this emphasis on people rather than on plot *All the King's Men* was ahead of its time. So too was Zinnemann's *The Men*, which was scripted by Carl Foreman and produced by Stanley Kramer. This film dealt frankly with the problems of a group of paraplegic patients who are undergoing treatment, and in particular with one among them who is unable at first to accept his paralysis until the combined influence of his fellow patients and his devoted girlfriend enables him to face his difficulties more positively. The part was played by a newcomer from the theatre, Marlon Brando, whose performance made it clear we had in him a new personality with particular powers for screen acting.

All the King's Men 1949. Director Robert Rossen
Broderick Crawford

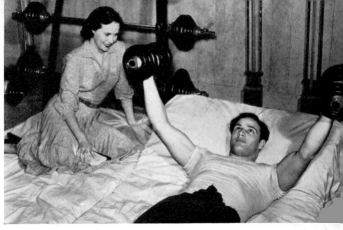

The Men 1950. Director Fred Zinnemann
Marlon Brando, Teresa Wright

The 1950s: background to the film industry

It was during the 1950s that the whole pattern of American production, distribution and exhibition changed. In the period 1950–
51, some 25,000 executives, creative artists and technicians were
engaged in making over 350 feature films annually. However, the
monolithic structure of the Hollywood companies which had
developed between the wars had already begun to experience the
first phase of erosion. The House Committee on Un-American
Activities investigating the infiltration of 'communism' into
motion pictures had held its first hearings in October 1947; from
this grew the notorious black list which by 1951 included the
names of many of Hollywood's best talents (especially screen
writers), and was the outcome of the infamous proceedings of
Senator Joseph McCarthy. When I visited Hollywood in 1952 the
whole profession seemed saturated with fear; no one seemed to
know who was going to play the informer in order to ingratiate
himself with authority, or against whom he was going to inform.
Whispering was everywhere. Films such as *The Best Years of Our
Lives* or even *Carrie* were thought to contain left-wing propaganda.
Soon an exodus to the cleaner air of Europe would begin, though
one highly-placed writer of impeccable political views spoke to
me of 'Mother Hollywood' in tones of the deepest sentiment.

If the un-American activity investigations of McCarthyism
prised open the first gap in Hollywood's foundations, another
rift was developing at the same time. The Anti-Trust Laws of

23

Carrie 1952. Director William Wyler
Laurence Olivier, Jennifer Jones

1950 broke up the so-called vertical integration of the film industry (that is, the combination of production and distribution with exhibition through circuits of cinemas owned by the same or interlocked companies). This meant that the great film production units, such as MGM and Paramount, lost their over-riding financial incentive to maintain the annual mass-production of films after they had lost control of the cinemas through which their product would automatically be shown. The greatest rift of all, however, was the extremely rapid popularisation of television, which by 1952 had begun to show marked signs of keeping the American public from going to the cinema. These figures reveal in the simplest terms what happened:

	NO. OF TV RECEIVERS IN UNITED STATES	NO. OF CINEMAS IN UNITED STATES	NO. OF AMERICAN FEATURE FILMS PRODUCED
1949	1½ m (1948, 200,000)	16,880 (excluding drive-ins)	363
1952	18 m	21,500 (4,500 drive-ins included)	278
1960	60 m	17,000 (4,700 drive-ins included)	211
1962	60 m	17,000 (4,700 drive-ins included)	138

The pattern of the 1950s was, therefore, one of radical adjustment to totally unforeseen conditions. 1952 saw the arrival of the new, enlarged screens—Cinerama and Cinemascope—and the consequent abandonment of the old, standard screen which had provided a universal norm for the cinemas of the world since the coming of sound. The old standard sound-film screen ratio was

1 : 1·22 ; the new standard screen-size approximates to 1 : 1·66 ; Cinemascope approximately 1 : 2·33 and Cinerama and Todd-AO approximately 1 : 2·0. During 1952, premature attempts were made to launch various quickly-devised systems providing a three-dimensional image, but they failed as they mostly deserved to do. This was not the way to compete with television, though the larger screens became much more exceptable as the quality of the image improved with time. The only way to draw audiences away from the television receiver was to make films of such a quality (in story, action, picture and star-value) that no television screen could rival them. Yet it took the best part of ten years of uncouth and bitter competition to discover that both television and the cinema possessed merits which were for the most part quite distinct. Each medium was eventually to learn much from the other, once they had come to terms with themselves and with the needs of their public.

As for the film studios in Hollywood, they became largely so much rented space where films either for the cinemas or television could be made by those with the financial backing. The day of the so-called 'independent' producer had come, though I shall not forget the ironic comments of one of the best-known of the American 'independents' when I used this term in his presence. Nevertheless, marked changes did take place in the nature of American feature film-making after the middle-1950s, and one of the reasons for this is, I think, the 'dispersion' of American film-makers over the face of America and the rest of the world leaving the old movie 'colony' to stew in the gravy of the ceaseless and profitable production of Westerns, crime and comedy series for television.

Hollywood had for the most part been bad for the film-maker. He had worked too far from the mainstream of American life in a highly competitive, utterly suburban back-water and in a mixture of strong sunshine and enervating smog, running the blind rat-race for the highest stakes in show-business. Hollywood basks in the endless exciting books exposing its 'evils', and even on occasion it has taken a bite at itself, as it did in *Sunset Boulevard* and more recently in *The Oscar*. But if some of the well-entrenched old-timers love their 'mother' Hollywood, many film-makers have a distaste for it, or, like Gavin Lambert, enjoy it because it gives them endless living copy for the exposure of its foibles.

In an area which has gathered together a phenomenal number of able and talented people, there is no collective culture, no 'background', nothing of the 'ambience' of a London, Paris, Rome or New York. Hollywood has ribbon-grown unnaturally—first because of the movies, later because other industries have moved into the area and created their own additional zones. Soon the studios themselves were looking for other outlets. Twentieth Century-Fox was lucky; they struck oil on the lot, and sold part of their estate for development.

The dispersion of feature film-makers meant that the independent producers could function much more nearly as individualists, and that the outstanding American films tended to stem from their work, which was admittedly on occasion made in Hollywood itself, to which the wanderer returned from time to time. But even the studio-sponsored films were made with a different intent. By the late 1950s Jerry Wald, one of the new-style producers who put Rouaults and Picassos on their office walls, was reported as saying: 'Mass audiences are hep now; there are 25 million college graduates. There's no such things as highbrow and lowbrow any more.' As a result it was he who produced films based on Faulkner's *The Sound and the Fury* and Lawrence's *Sons and Lovers*, and he even bought an option on Joyce's *Ulysses*. Dilys Powell, visiting Hollywood in 1960, quotes Stanley Kubrick, one of the most influential of the younger generation of independents, as saying: 'The source of the supremacy of the majors was their power to make money. When they stopped making money, they sent for the independent producers.'

However, Hollywood has become to a large extent the servant rather than the master of television film-making, and it is estimated that over half its current 20,000 employees work exclusively to supply television with films. The hatred of the new medium was so great among top executives that for the most part they neglected to jump on the bandwagon which it offered them. An exception to this was Columbia's formation (from the New York office) of Screen Gems Inc., to handle television production; this subsidiary was later to make vast profits and so help to support the impoverished parent company; another exception was Walt Disney's lucrative association as early as 1954 with American Broadcasting Company Television. MCA (Music Corporation of America), a former talent agency, turned into a powerful production group for television, buying up Universal's studios. By the mid-1950s, the large companies became for the most part battle-grounds for take-over bids by various financial giants emerging from the shadows of other industries.

But the American film industry, receiving economic blood transfusions from outside sources and income from the many-headed and ever-hungry monster of television, is by no means dead though it is in effect ruled from New York. Jack Valenti, a former aide to President Johnson, became in 1966, with the President's personal support, head of the Motion Picture Association of America. To strengthen his hand, Valenti took as his legal adviser Louis Nizer, one of the most astute lawyers in American show-business. It is to Jack Valenti, as well as to the independents, that we owe the current relaxation of the forbidding American censor code. He is also well aware of the technical backwardness of the American studios, and their crying need to catch up with the kind of research which makes the other industries of the United States a generation ahead of the motion picture industry. The signs are that Hollywood is on the turn towards making more films for the cinemas.

A senior man working for Hollywood on the production of a successful series may earn as much as $100,000 a year, but the fortunate independent producer, who uses Hollywood only when he feels like it, belongs to the $500,000 a year bracket, and upwards.* The independents, usually producer-directors concerned to make one film at a time, have for the past decade been moving about the world according to the particular needs of the subject on which they are working. In any case, costs in Europe run, on average, about one-third cheaper than in the United States. Some of these independents left early for political reasons, such as Carl Foreman and Joseph Losey, both of whom made new careers for themselves in Britain. Other independents have worked repeatedly in Britain and in other European centres for film-making—for example, John Huston, Stanley Kubrick, Otto

* The costs of a Hollywood film are customarily divided into 'above' and 'below' line outgoings. Above the line stands the cost of the 'property' or subject, the screenplay, the producer's, director's and actors' fees; below the line expenditure covers all the costs of actual production, studio overheads, technicians' wages, the costs of all raw materials used, film stock and processing. Both below and above line costs vary considerably. A senior technician on the studio floor in Hollywood earns, perhaps, $700 to $1,000 a week; a good lighting cameraman earns probably $1,000 to $5,000 a week. Average production costs for Hollywood features rose from $400,000 in 1941 to $1,500,000 in 1963. Richard D. Zanuck, son of Darryl Zanuck and Vice-President in charge of production for Twentieth Century-Fox, claimed in 1967 that a film costing $1 million less than ten years previously would now cost $2½ million, and would have to show a return of $7½ million to break even.

Hollywood does well out of its sale of old films for screening on television. In 1967, for example, United Artists agreed with NBC–TV to let them have 55 old features at the rate of $2 million a film, maximum three screenings. Price can reach $5 million for a single showing of a major feature film on American television.

Preminger, Nicholas Ray, Anthony Mann, Jules Dassin and Orson Welles. Their films, therefore, are often classed not as American (which they may well remain in style and treatment) but as British or Italian or Spanish, as the case may be.

As far as the purely box-office picture is concerned, there has been a growing movement in favour of the production of the 'block-buster'—the big picture whose inflated budget ensures a screen loaded with spectacle, whether in the tradition of the musical, the costume epic (biblical or classical), or the films offering large-scale action from nearer contemporary times—for example war films such as *The Battle of the Bulge*. Budgets range from over $3 million for *Spartacus* (1960, Stanley Kubrick) and $5 million for *Ben-Hur* (1959, William Wyler) to the record (so far) of over $45 million for *Cleopatra* (though this fantastic total was hardly contemplated at the outset). Blockbusters of a reasonable quality usually retrieve their outlay and make handsome profits. *South Pacific* ran unbroken for several years in London's Dominion cinema; its director, Joshua Logan, simply could not account for this degree of success when we discussed it. (As much will be expected of his latest film, *Camelot*.) It had grossed in all over $16 million by 1962, though the champion still remained the pre-war *Gone with the Wind*, which by the same year had grossed out of its endless revivals over $41 million. *The Sound of Music* was seen by some 23 million people in Britain, and grossed more than £7 million in that country alone. 'I have seen it six times and you are not human if you do not enjoy watching it,' said a woman enthusiast in Dudley. One lady, Miss Alice Jackson, claimed to have seen it 121 times.

Ben-Hur 1959. Director William Wyler
Stephen Boyd

Camelot 1967. Director Joshua Logan
Franco Nero

The epic in its proper sense should be a film with a sufficient historical canvas to allow the larger human values to emerge. Film epics tend to belittle these larger themes by expending screentime on the more puerile relationships (sexual or political) imposed on their leading characters; the films become inflated melodramas backed by scenes of action performed by vast crowds. Among the epics of higher quality have been: *War and Peace* (Vidor, 1955–6), *Spartacus* (Kubrick, 1960), and *Barabbas*

War and Peace 1955–56. Director King Vidor
Henry Fonda

(Richard Fleischer, 1962). Samuel Bronston, an ambitious producer of taste who was born in Russia and educated at the
Sorbonne, has made several spectacular films in Spain, among
them *El Cid* and *The Fall of the Roman Empire* (directed by Anthony
Mann and shown in 1961 and 1963 respectively), and *King of
Kings* (Nicholas Ray, 1963). *Lawrence of Arabia* (directed by
David Lean, 1962) was produced by the American Sam Spiegel
as a British film; it is reputed to have cost some £4½ million, but
there is no question that it was immensely profitable. Yet it, like
some of the other films mentioned above, represented in many
respects a departure from the primal innocence and absence of
sophistication which characterised the traditional American
spectacular film. It was made to meet and satisfy the somewhat
changing tastes of urban cinemagoers in the most profitable parts
of the world. It was the product of the middle generation of
international film-makers. But before we consider how and why
these changes came about, we must consider the work of the
traditionalists in American film-making, on whose talents the
whole foundation of Hollywood had originally rested.

The traditionalists

Some of America's finest directors are content to work within the accepted patterns of the cinema. To a considerable extent they have created these patterns themselves, giving stature to convention. Several of them were born in the 1890s, including Henry King, Lewis Milestone, Henry Hathaway, William Wellman, Howard Hawks, King Vidor, George Cukor, John Ford and Alfred Hitchcock.

Henry King (born 1892) is the senior director by age among the traditionalists; his post-war films include *Twelve o'Clock High* (1950), a taut, precise film in which Gregory Peck appears as a senior officer in the American Army Air Force whose ruthless attempt to re-discipline an over-strained bomber group finally leads to mental collapse, and an outstanding Western, *The Gunfighter* (1951).

Lewis Milestone, who was born in Russia in 1895 and went to America in his teens, worked initially with Thomas Ince, Henry King and Mack Sennett. His film of World War II, *A Walk in the Sun* (1945), was a deeply-felt, humane study of a small detachment of men sent on a difficult mission to capture a strongpoint.

A Walk in the Sun 1945. Director Lewis Milestone
Dana Andrews

The film was more concerned with these men as individuals—their relationships, their sense of discipline as members of a closely-knit fighting unit—than it was with their carefully calculated conduct of a dangerous action. It was one of the best of the American war films—quiet, laconic, unpretentious and with a special, succinct shapeliness which gave it a slowly mounting tension. Milestone was later to direct several notable films, including *Oceans Eleven* (1960, with Frank Sinatra) and *Mutiny on the Bounty* (1962).

Henry Hathaway's special contribution to the post-war cinema was, as we have seen, in the field of the documentary crime film; he was later to direct, among many more conventional films, a part of *How the West Was Won* (1963), which developed the spectacular medium of Cinerama for a large-scale historical action film.

William Wellman has been described by Kevin Brownlow as 'an authentic figure of the Old West; tall and lean, with a tough, weatherbeaten face and a voice exactly like John Wayne'. Some of his early films have become a part of American screen history—

The Story of GI Joe 1945. Director William Wellman
Burgess Meredith

films such as *Wings* (1927), *Nothing Sacred* (1937) and *The Oxbow Incident* (1942). If he has a recurrent speciality it is war films, among which *The Story of GI Joe* (1945) remains outstanding; it starred Burgess Meredith as a war-hardened but sympathetic correspondent sharing a tough life with the American GIs in order to send home honest, first-hand reports from the fighting fronts.

Howard Hawks, like Wellman, was a flier; he became a racing pilot of some distinction. Like other highly professional Hollywood directors, he worked in most of the *genre* forms familiar on the American screen—from crime films (*Scarface*, 1932, and *The Big Sleep*, 1946) and war subjects (*Dawn Patrol*, 1930, and *Sergeant York*, 1941) to musicals (*Gentlemen Prefer Blondes*, 1953), Westerns (*Red River,* 1948, *The Big Sky*, 1952, *Rio Bravo*, 1959, and *El Dorado*, 1967) and farcical comedy with a disillusioned, even sadistic humour (*I Was a Male War Bride*, 1949). *Red River*, with John Wayne, Montgomery Clift and Joanne Dru, is one of his best films exposing the violence beneath the moral differences between father and son which come to a head during

Red River 1948. Director Howard Hawks

a hazardous cattle drive from Texas to Missouri during the pioneer period. The film filled in the whole economic and social background of the cattle trade of the period, and has all the immense energy characteristic of Hawks's best work. His Westerns, though much harsher and more realistic than Ford's, are conceived on the grand scale, and he also takes account of the hard impact of women on men, a relationship which Ford always treats romantically.

King Vidor was trained in much the same school as Milestone; after working in newsreel he became an assistant to Griffith and Ince. His career, like that of all the directors of this group, spans the greater part of Hollywood's history; and in 1953 he published an autobiography, *A Tree is a Tree*, in which he describes the rapidly evolving pattern of American film-making and the problems that resulted from the growing elaboration and costliness of production. His early films, which include *The Big Parade* (1925), *The Crowd* (1927) and *Our Daily Bread* (1934), showed his ability to handle the large-scale action which appeals strongly to Hollywood's sense of *panache*; and this developed in his later, post-war films, with the vast production in Italy of *War and Peace* (1955) and *Solomon and Sheba* (1959). He also made a strange film, *Ruby Gentry* (1952) with Jennifer Jones, Charlton Heston and Karl Malden. This story of the backwoods centres round Ruby, a half-wild girl, and her divided desire for two men which leads to violence not only between them but in the remote community where they live. The film is remarkable not so much for its novelettish story as for its disturbing atmosphere and the extraordinary character which Jennifer Jones develops out of Ruby.

George Cukor's films show great concern for his actors. His earlier subjects (including W. C. Fields in *David Copperfield*, 1934, Garbo in *Camille*, 1936, and Katharine Hepburn in *The Philadelphia Story*, 1940) all revealed his capacity to obtain star performances from highly individual artists in subjects carefully chosen to exploit their star qualities. He has said: 'I achieve practically all my film effects through the actors and actresses. I'm interested in people, in the way they behave. Other directors get their effects by photographing doorknobs turning and that sort of thing. I like to concentrate on the actors' faces.' He is able to impose his own discipline on players who are normally difficult to handle. In his post-war films, his stars have included: Judy Holliday in *Born Yesterday* (1950), Jean Simmons and Spencer

Born Yesterday 1950. Director George Cukor
Broderick Crawford, Judy Holliday

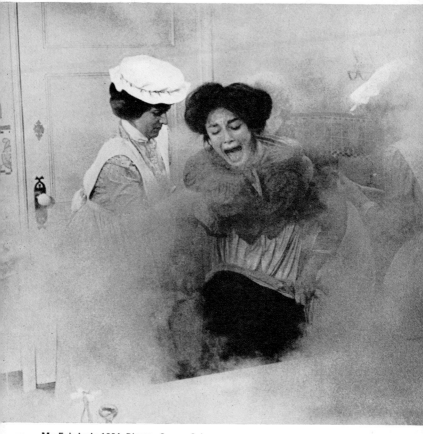

My Fair Lady 1964. Director George Cukor
Audrey Hepburn

Opposite:
Fort Apache 1948. Director John Ford
John Wayne, Henry Fonda

Tracy in *The Actress* (1953), Judy Garland in *A Star is Born*
(1954), Anna Magnani in *Wild is the Wind* (1957), Sophia
Loren in *Heller in Pink Tights* (1959) and Audrey Hepburn in
My Fair Lady (1964). He is as successful as he can make his stars
successful in mainly conventional subjects.

The work of Ford and Hitchcock, although firmly linked to the
broad and colourful tradition of box-office entertainment, has

in each case a personal stature which gives them the almost unique distinction of being well known to the general public as directors. Yet, while Hitchcock has always enjoyed taking part in his own publicity (more particularly through his trailers and television appearances), Ford remains initially uncommunicative. Both are prolific workers with a sure eye for the subject which suits their outstanding talents, though both are capable of stepping aside and making mistakes now and then—as Hitchcock did with the static, trundling, long-take scenes in *Rope* (1949). They are the supreme examples of the artist-artisan in film-making, men whose whole life is bound up with a constant stream of work. Ford's record will not fall far short of 200 films when he eventually retires. Hitchcock's output of meticulously planned productions (his fiftieth was completed in 1965) has averaged well over a film a year since the time when Michael Balcon, only three

My Darling Clementine 1946. Director John Ford
Henry Fonda, John Wayne

years his senior, launched him on his career in Britain in the mid-1920s. Hitchcock did not leave to work in America until 1939.

Hitchcock remains the imperturbable entertainer without any particular national ties, though his recognised base has been the United States for almost thirty years. Ford remains essentially the indigenous American film-maker, with an innate response to the old-fashioned, isolationist values of the far West. Ford's post-war films—which include *My Darling Clementine* (1946), *Fort Apache* (1948), *She Wore a Yellow Ribbon* (1949), *Wagonmaster* (1950), *The Sun Shines Bright* (1953), *The Searchers* (1956), *The Horse Soldiers* (1959), *The Man Who Shot Liberty Valance* (1961) and *Cheyenne Autumn* (1964)—complete the image of the West which he has created with a kind of rugged loving-care since *Stagecoach* in 1939. Perhaps only direct, physical contact with the spacious landscapes of that territory

My Darling Clementine 1946. Director John Ford
Henry Fonda

(including Ford's favourite Monument Valley, Utah, with its towering mesas) can excite in the non-American something of the deeply-romantic response to place and period which is evident in all of Ford's Western films. These locations conjure up for him, as he does for us on the screen, the great legend of the West created a century ago as part of the history of American national expansion. The grandeur of his vision is more than sufficient to contain the lesser romantic strains which run through it—the last-minute rescues by the faithful cavalry, the nationalist sentimentality, the Irish-American tear for hearth and home. Ford has his own line in blarney. But his sentiment is always turning into real

Wagonmaster 1950. Director John Ford

tenderness. Counterpointing this old-fashioned largeness of feeling is the technical discipline of his observation of what makes up a location and its people. This is as sharp and exact in its cumulative detail (for example, the prostitute's funeral in *The Sun Shines Bright*) as the scenes of violent action, to which most of Ford's films eventually lead, are brilliantly organised from their original shot break-down to their re-assembly on the cutting-bench. Ford, therefore, is the master-craftsman who knows every inch of play in his medium, from slow tempo to shock-cut. But behind this mastery is Ford the artist—warmly responsive to the American people he knows and to the tradition out of which their remoter

communities have been raised, the drama of their aspirations set mostly to their own folk-music, for which Ford has such a pronounced taste. His conservatism has led him to keep to the same actors in many of his films—notably, of course, John Wayne, Henry Fonda and Victor McLaglen—and to re-use such actresses as Mildred Natwick, Maureen O'Hara, Dorothy Jordan and Joanne Dru.

Ford's films tend to involve the larger human issues—love, loyalty, the family, birth, death, the establishment of law and order in the face of the outlaw, morality and immorality, the founding of new territories for the nation at the cost of the greatest hardship, bloodshed and the subjugation of the Red Indian (who is shown as a proud, bitter, cunning and cruel foe). Ford's personal response to the people who live continuously in the immediate

The Horse Soldiers 1959. Director John Ford
John Wayne

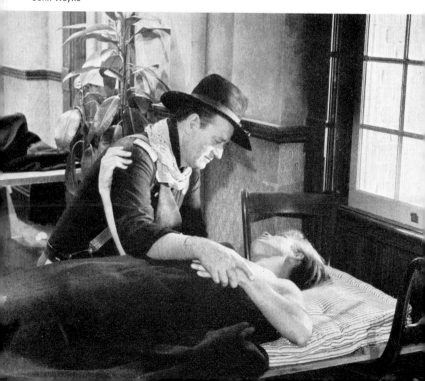

light and shadow of these things is what makes his films so often rise into a form of poetry, at once both lyric and epic, which stands firm against any taint of contemporary sophistication.

Hitchcock is, as we have seen, far more communicative than Ford. But the last thing he wants is to be mistaken for some sort of intellectual, however much he may be entertained by the admiration his work excites in the intellectual followers of the cinema. He has explained often enough how he sets about the realisation of a film. Here he is writing in 1949: 'One of the main problems facing a film director is how to convey his ideas to his technicians, actors and cameraman. How to ensure that what he sees behind his eyes shall be realised in front of them, by himself and his fellow-technicians, on the screen's white rectangle . . When I read a story I visualise it as a sequence of dramatic incidents. And I have naturally trained myself to see these incidents in terms of pictures limited to the confines of a frame of film. Immediately I have read the story to be filmed, I grab a notepad on which are roneoed empty rectangles representing frames of film. Into the rectangles go ovals to depict the faces of the players in the scene visualised—occupying exactly the positions in which the camera's eye shall see those faces when the scene is to be shot . . . For every change of camera set-up there's a new drawing.'

Perhaps he enjoys disquieting his more profound interpreters. In various interviews he has said: 'Really, I'm not very interested in subjects and characters: only in making films. It's like asking a still-life painter if he's interested in apples; the only answer is "Not particularly, but you've got to paint something." Well, it's the same with me; I've got to make films about something, but I don't attach all that importance to what it is . . . I decide on a subject, hire a writer and just talk to him about it for several weeks until I think he knows what I want. Then I send him off to write a draft script, and when he comes back I start pulling it to pieces and re-arranging, always with the writer standing by. Then I myself re-dictate the whole final script from beginning to end. At that stage I have virtually the whole film in my head, and change and improvise very little on the set . . . Acting's for the stage; all you want on the screen is for actors to be themselves, not to create characters.' Talking on television in 1964, he made the point that 'the assembly of pieces of film to create fright is the essential part of my job', and that the fright caused has to be basic and universal, recollections in adults of the kind of fright they experienced when children. He likes, he said, to excite the kind of

Rear Window 1953. Director Alfred Hitchcock
James Stewart

screaming which happens on a switchback railway, which is not
the scream of *real* horror experienced in *real* life. A good scream,
like a good cry, is good for you. He added that he believed in
'putting the horror in the *mind* of the audience and not necessarily
on the screen'. *Psycho*, he has said, was made as a joke, developing from the overt horror of the murder in the shower to horror
which is increasingly suggested rather than shown.

   Now it is evident that this kind of master-technician's approach
to the cinema is far removed from the rationalising of motive
which certain critics discover in Hitchcock's films. He may like

44

North by Northwest 1959. Director Alfred Hitchcock
Cary Grant

to think of his films as technical experiments in entertainment,
many of them of a kind which appeal to his lightly sadistic sense
of humour. But his films necessarily deal in the permutations and
combinations of human relationships, with the eternal puzzles in
human nature which accompany manifestations of loyalty and
disloyalty, innocence and guilt—the complexities of motivation
which make nothing in the end quite what it seems. But of the
patterns of behaviour developed in films such as *Rear Window*
(1953), *The Trouble with Harry* (1956, one of the most fascinating
of his films but, in fact, one of the least successful with the public),

Psycho 1960. Director Alfred Hitchcock

Vertigo (1958), *North by Northwest* (1959) and *Psycho* (1960), a psychological framework of some interest and even significance can no doubt be constructed. After all, as one intellectual critic of *The Birds* (1963) has put it: 'The ambiguity of the film's meaning is a prime virtue'. So we can take it where we like from there.

Such, then, are the leading film-makers in America who, by 1950, were all over 50 years of age. Their total achievement in the main conventions of film entertainment is on such a level that it can be said they set most of the standards by which we still judge the traditional American cinema. Their immediate successors —born at the turn of the century or soon afterwards—were to include men who were in various ways to disturb these conventions. They include the American-born directors Preston Sturges (who died in 1959), William Wyler, George Stevens, John Huston and Anthony Mann (who died suddenly on location in Berlin in 1967), as well as others who came originally from Europe: Anatole Litvak, Billy Wilder and Fred Zinnemann, all of whom settled in the United States during the 1930s. Litvak's span, for example, has been considerable—from the pre-war *Confessions of a Nazi Spy* (1939) and the post-war *Sorry, Wrong Number* (1948) to the recent Franco-British production, *Night of the Generals* (1966).

Sorry, Wrong Number 1948. Director Anatole Litvak
Barbara Stanwyck

The formulae of film entertainment had in any case to be disturbed to match the changing demands of post-war audiences. It is only relatively true to say that the more these box-office formulae change, the more they remain the same. Audiences want perpetually to be moved, surprised, shocked, astonished and impressed, but the kinds of situation and the kinds of character calculated to achieve this change continually. Gradually the older techniques become too familiar, too easy to forecast, and writers, directors and actors, as well as those responsible for the design and appearance of a film, have to be continually resourceful in keeping their work in the van of these changes in public taste, anticipating and even creating them when they can. However, a few great directors, such as Hitchcock, are able to re-surface their films in the modern style while retaining the essential pattern of their traditional plot manoeuvres; while Ford (like the late Cecil B. de Mille) remains monolithically in the past, in any case setting most of his films back in historical period.

The newer men

Among the newer men, whose first films as directors did not for the most part begin to appear until the 1940s, Delmer Daves has remained closest to tradition. He began as a property-boy working for James Cruze on *The Covered Wagon*, and he knows well both the territories and the people he films, including the Indians; his grandfather fought in the Civil War and travelled on the wagon trains.

Daves is a man completely absorbed and happy in his work, free of any contaminating sophistication, and more dedicated to making the Western location film than any other form. I once spent two weeks in his company in the Argentine, and from this learnt at first hand what appeals most to the film-maker who is wholly involved in the Western tradition. Daves is prolific because he can think of nothing better than to be out at work, prospecting his locations in the early morning sun before his technicians arrive. Though he scripted many films in the 1930s, including *The Petrified Forest*, and later directed several war films (such as *Destination Tokyo*, 1943, and *Task Force*, 1949), his most consistently good work has been in the mainstream of the true Western, in which men become a real part of the place where they work and live—like the heroes of *3.10 to Yuma* (1957) and *Cowboy* (1958), or the people in the ranch-communities in *Jubal* (1956) and in the mining community in *The Hanging Tree* (1959). Daves's sympathy for and understanding of the Red Indian was shown in *Broken Arrow* (1950); his interest in Western history as distinct from legend in *Drumbeat* (1954); his command of hard

Opposite:
Broken Arrow 1950. Director Delmer Daves
James Stewart, Debra Paget

3.10 To Yuma 1952. Director Delmer Daves
Van Heflin, Glenn Ford

Opposite:
Last Train from Gun Hill 1959. Director John Sturges
Kirk Douglas, Anthony Quinn

action, as distinct from community activity, in *The Last Wagon* (1957), which tells the story of the survivors of a wagon-train that has been attacked by the Apaches. Like Ford, Daves is concerned with basic human values and loyalties, with love and friendship and the self-seeking which destroys them. The humour and the tensions of *3.10 to Yuma*, with its restrained, subtle inter-play of character, shows Daves's work at its best. John Sturges

(*Bad Day at Black Rock,* 1954; *Gunfight at the O.K. Corral,* 1957; *Last Train from Gun Hill* (1959); *Hallelujah Trail,* 1964) and the late Anthony Mann (*The Naked Spur,* 1952, and *The Man from Laramie,* 1954) also added, as we shall see, to the development of the Western.

It was, however, the newer men who were responsible for the erosion of the legend of the 'heroic' West, and who began to concentrate on the social shortcomings of its tradition of rugged individualism. The lynch-law of Wellman's great film of the war period, *The Oxbow Incident* (or *Strange Incident*, 1942) had shown the uglier aspects of a small community unable to resist

Opposite:
The Gunfighter 1951. Director Henry King
Gregory Peck

Hallelujah Trail 1964. Director John Sturges

Shane 1953. Director George Stevens
Van Heflin, Alan Ladd

Opposite:
High Noon 1952. Director Fred Zinnemann
Gary Cooper

On pages 56/57
Cat Ballou 1965. Director Elliot Silverstein
Lee Marvin, Jane Fonda

the pressures of men (representing both the 'outlaws' and the 'respectable') who were determined to resist any kind of community law; this film had the slow-moving inevitability of classical tragedy. So had Henry King's *The Gunfighter*. Among other films which attacked the heroic tradition of the West were Fred Zinnemann's celebrated film, *High Noon* (1952, produced by Stanley Kramer and scripted by Carl Foreman), George Stevens's *Shane* (1953), William Wyler's *The Big Country* (1958) and John Huston's *The Unforgiven* (1959).

High Noon, set back in 1865, shows how the morale of a small town in the West collapses when a killer who has terrorised the place is known to be returning. The townsfolk withdraw support from their Marshall, played by Gary Cooper, even on the day of his wedding to a Quaker girl, played by Grace Kelly. He has to face the killer alone in the deserted streets. Van Heflin, in *Shane*, plays

a homesteader in Wyoming at the turn of the century. He and his family are terrorised by outlaws whose black-clad gunman, Wilson (Jack Palance), is finally killed by Shane, a fugitive gunfighter who befriends the all-but defenceless family. In this film the killings are vicious and real, but the atmosphere is sustained magnificently and the situation is treated realistically except, perhaps, for the slightly romantic, mysterious-stranger figure of Shane himself. (Other films which introduced the 'purposeful stranger' character were John Sturges's *Bad Day at Black Rock,* with Spencer Tracy as the stranger, and Anthony Mann's *The Man from Laramie,* in which James Stewart arrives in a small town in New Mexico to look for the white man who sold the guns to the Apaches with which his brother had been killed). *The Big Country* exposed the violent feuding which could extend to murder only too easily when rival claims (in this case to water rights) eliminate all human reason; the film featured Gregory Peck as the honest man seeking in vain to bring about peace. Huston's *The Unforgiven*, set in the post Civil War period, featured Audrey Hepburn as a girl suspected of being an Indian rescued from a massacre. The whole of the small community in which she lives think of little else but how to get rid of her; she is protected solely by Ben, son of the man who is said to have saved her as a child, but the ostracism leads in the end to bloodshed.

The 'heroic' Western also suffered change by being given either a psychological or a sexual slant. Westerns were not always quite so 'torrid' as King Vidor's over-sensationalised *Duel in the Sun* (1946, with Jennifer Jones), which was described at the time as 'lust in the dust', nor so impassioned as Vidor's *Ruby Gentry* and Nicholas Ray's *Johnny Guitar* (1953). (Marlon Brando's very way-out Western-by-the-sea, *One-Eyed Jacks* (1961), will be mentioned later.) *Johnny Guitar* featured Joan Crawford as Vienna, the owner of a gambling joint in pioneer Arizona, and ended in a gunfight between Vienna and another woman, who suspects one of Vienna's lovers to have killed her brother. Johnny Guitar is an outlaw with whom she has a special love-hate relationship, but he stands by her when the townsfolk finally turn against her. In Anthony Mann's *The Naked Spur* (1952), James Stewart reappears as a man who eventually retires from the whole business of trailing the outlaw and claiming his just reward, largely because he falls in love with the outlaw's girlfriend, who helps him kill her former lover. Robert Aldrich's *Apache* (1954) looked at the invasion of the West from the point of view of an Indian 'resistance' fighter, Geronimo, played by Burt Lancaster. The film ends on a distinctly pacifist note. Other films which in one way or another exposed the Western legend were David Miller's *Lonely are the Brave* (1962) and Elliot Silverstein's delightful burlesque, *Cat Ballou* (1965).

Audiences for American films had come to rely on the various accepted species, the hall-marked forms of entertainment recognisable from the moment you set eyes on the publicity or read the first words of the critics' notices. The only way in which to break up the moulds in which all these films were cast was to crack them from inside—to give (for example) the film about the gangster a social or even a political twist, or to introduce deeper psychological factors into the dramas of love or war, or raise sociological or even psychological issues in the Western. The results were not always happy; there were often signs of strain, of too great a burden of 'purpose', too much 'significance' being placed upon forms of entertainment unfitted to carry the load.

Changes, too, were to take place in the conception of the hero

Bus Stop 1956. Director Joshua Logan
Marilyn Monroe

and heroine. Many of the prominent stars of the 1950s presented the screen with characters who were ambivalent, replacing the clear-cut and easy-to-identify heroes and heroines of the past. In fact, the very words hero and heroine ceased to be applicable to the kind of people portrayed by Marlon Brando, James Dean or Marilyn Monroe, to take the most obvious. Side by side with these newer personalities, the established stars retained their success. The top money-making stars of the period 1950–60 included John Wayne, Dean Martin and Jerry Lewis (as a team), James Stewart, William Holden, Cary Grant, Rock Hudson, Glenn Ford, Betty Grable, Grace Kelly, Debbie Reynolds, Doris Day and Elizabeth Taylor.

The newer directors, however, the men of the middle generation, seemed content to establish their individuality by cracking the moulds rather than actually breaking free from the established *genres* of Hollywood entertainment. At the time, however, the appearance of these cracks seemed like some sort of revolution, and the films which resulted during the later 1940s and early 1950s seemed fresh and invigorating. The directors involved included in particular Billy Wilder, Joseph Mankiewicz, William Wyler, George Stevens, Anthony Mann, Richard Brooks, Otto Preminger, Stanley Kramer, Robert Rossen, Daniel Mann, Robert Aldrich, Laslo Benedek, Preston Sturges, John Huston, Orson Welles, Fred Zinnemann, Nicholas Ray and Robert Wise.

These men, all of them individualists, shared in the establishment of the post-war movement towards greater realism, but they seldom, if ever, made films which stayed within the plain, post-war, documentary style. These directors were story-tellers with their own stylish differences, most of them strong and assured, at least on the surface. In some cases this stylishness emerged in films with a certain bizarre quality. Among the best of the earlier films of this kind were Billy Wilder's *Double Indemnity* (1944) and *Sunset Boulevard* (1950), and John Huston's *The Treasure of Sierra Madre* (1947) and *The Asphalt Jungle* (1950). These films made use of the 'effects' of realism, but the situations in which the characters found themselves were always of an extreme nature, involving tension, violence and unusual, even threatening, forms of characterisation with their own dramatic 'mystery'. So, while the general appearance of these films seemed to link them with the new realism, this surface credibility was merely being used to offset the dramatic strangeness of the situations—a technique, of course, often employed by Hitchcock.

Sunset Boulevard 1950. Director Billy Wilder
Gloria Swanson , William Holden

Wilder's work was among the most striking. 'People out front want to hear what the actors are saying and understand the meaning of the plot,' he has said. He is against aestheticism in the cinema. 'We shoot only from the angles that help us tell the story. To me a director who uses phenomenal neck-craning set-ups, beautiful pictures everywhere, isn't worth a damn.' His sense of humour burned holes alike in his scripts and on the set. Wilder is Jewish and was born an Austrian; he worked as a successful scriptwriter in Berlin until 1933, and arrived in America the following year with no knowledge of English. His talent as a writer eventually brought him for a period into partnership with Charles Brackett, with whom he enjoyed many outstanding successes, including *Bluebeard's Eighth Wife*, *Ninotchka* and *The Lost Weekend*. Then he turned director, scripting all his films (often in association with the writer I. A. L. Diamond, another immigrant) from *Double Indemnity* and *Sunset Boulevard* to *The Seven Year Itch* (1955), *Some Like It Hot* (1959), *The Apartment* (1960;

Opposite:
Some Like It Hot 1959. Director Billy Wilder
Jack Lemmon, Marilyn Monroe

The Apartment 1960. Director Billy Wilder
Jack Lemmon, Shirley MacLaine

Ace in the Hole 1951. Director Billy Wilder
Kirk Douglas

a film which won three Oscars), *Kiss Me Stupid* (1964) and
Meet Whiplash Willy (1967). Through his continuous success he
has earned the right to his independence as a writer–director–
producer who challenges alike the censor, romantic attitudes to
women and any generally accepted sense of good taste. He has

been attacked for his nihilistic cynicism, for his inhumane characterisation, for his caustic portrait of modern society. It would seem fairer to say that his cynicism alike in *Double Indemnity*, *Ace in the Hole* (*The Big Carnival*, 1951), *Sunset Boulevard* or *The Apartment* is directed against the ever-increasing pretention and opportunism of a complex, egotistical, urbanised society in which everyone but yourself is on the make. Wilder expends his coruscating humour with all the relish of a showman who knows the exact measure of his satiric strength. One might claim that his ironic, 'black' comedies had been anticipated by Charles Chaplin in *Monsieur Verdoux* (1947).

Monsieur Verdoux 1947. Director Charles Chaplin
Charles Chaplin

Wilder is by no means alone in making this form of satiric attack. American filmgoers, like American fiction readers, seem to have become masochistic in their taste for the ceaseless exposure of the worst evils in their society, a taste which is speading now to Europe.

I first met Joseph Mankiewicz in New York in 1952, when he was about to make *Julius Caesar*. By then he had made the Oscar-winning *A Letter to Three Wives* (1948; three American wives endure a period of suspense when they each receive a letter from a mutual girl friend telling them she has run off with *one* of their husbands) and *All About Eve* (1950, with Bette Davis). *Julius*

All About Eve 1950. Director Joseph Mankiewicz
Bette Davis, Gary Merrill

Julius Caesar 1953. Director Joseph Mankiewicz
Marlon Brando

Caesar (1953) was produced by that highly literate stage and film producer, John Houseman, whose productions also include Max Ophüls' *Letter from an Unknown Woman,* Robert Wise's *Executive Suite* and John Frankenheimer's *All Fall Down.* Later Mankiewicz was to make *The Barefoot Contessa* (1954, with Ava Gardner), *Guys and Dolls* (1955) and *The Honeypot* (1967). And, of course, he undertook the agonising task of re-writing and at the same time directing *Cleopatra* (1963). (The story of some part of this astonishing enterprise is told by Walter Wanger, the film's producer, in his book *My Life with Cleopatra,* a very nice example of Hollywood self-expression). Mankiewicz has claimed that many of his films deal with people who 'have a quality of desperation in their lives', and that he likes to work with stars to match, especially women, to whom he normally gives the best acting parts. It is evident that Mankiewicz believes in strong, sophisticated, even alarmist subjects, in which women appear

Opposite:
Cleopatra 1963. Director Joseph Mankiewicz
Elizabeth Taylor

Guys and Dolls 1955. Director Joseph Mankiewicz
Vivian Blaine

The Heiress 1949. Director William Wyler
Olivia de Havilland and Montgomery Clift

mostly as predators. *Julius Caesar* is an exception; it was shot virtually in the order of action on a large, composite, outdoor set, using a minimum of reaction shots in order to concentrate attention on the speaker. The characters, more particularly of Caesar and Antony (played by Louis Calhern and Marlon Brando) were treated in a near-contemporary style modelled on the Nazi leaders.

The Loudest Whisper (The Children's Hour) 1962. Director William Wyler
Shirley MacLaine, Audrey Hepburn

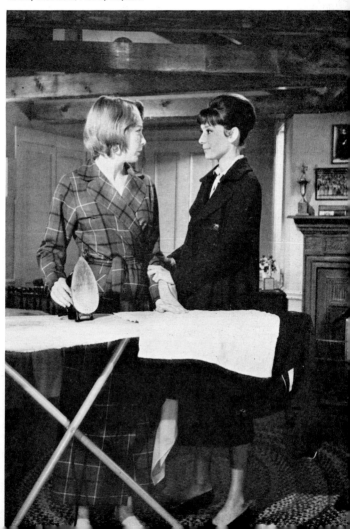

William Wyler (whom Carl Laemmle invited to emigrate from Europe to the United States to work for Universal) describes his earliest, unlisted films as 'just awful'; many of them were two-reel Westerns. This was during the 1920s. A decade later he was directing such films as *Dodsworth*, *Dead End* and *Wuthering Heights*. Post-war, after *The Best Years of Our Lives* (1946), came such films as *The Heiress* (1949), *Carrie* (1952), *Ben-Hur* (1959), *The Loudest Whisper* (*The Children's Hour*, 1962) and *The Collector* (1965), as well as *The Big Country*, which has already been mentioned. *The Heiress*, adapted by Ruth and Augustus Goetz from their play taken from Henry James's novel, *Washington Square*, contained a sensitive portrait by Olivia de Havilland of the girl who loses her lover; she was supported by Ralph Richardson as the father and Montgomery Clift as the faithless young man. *Carrie* also featured a young girl, played by Jennifer Jones, who loses everything she really wants in life, though it is the middle-aged restaurant proprietor who befriends her, played by Laurence Olivier, who is in the end reduced to penury through his infatuation. In *The Collector*, Wyler obtained the same meticulous performances from Terence Stamp and Samantha Eggar as a potential psychopath and the girl whom he imprisons in order to

The Collector 1965. Director William Wyler
Terence Stamp, Samantha Eggar

A Place in the Sun 1951. Director George Stevens
Elizabeth Taylor, Montgomery Clift

make her fall in love with him. Wyler is an academician in screen portraiture.

George Stevens—his principal films include *A Place in the Sun* (1951, adapted from Dreiser's *An American Tragedy*), *Shane* (1953), *Giant* (1956) and *The Diary of Anne Frank* (1958)— is another director whose talents lie in powerful and very emotive forms of stylised realism. That is, the details observed are all

The Diary of Anne Frank 1958. Director George Stevens
Millie Perkins

Giant 1956. Director George Stevens
James Dean

realistic, authentic to the location, but the manner in which they
are used is artificially developed to achieve highly seasoned
dramatic effects. We have already considered *Shane*, one of the
most effective of the post-war Westerns. Stevens was reared
hard in motion pictures—writing gags, working as a camera
operator, even directing Laurel and Hardy shorts; yet he de-
parts from the 'dynamic' American tradition by refusing to
hurry his films along. In both *Shane* and *Giant* he dwells on the

tensions, the violences in the story with a slow accumulation of atmosphere, though many moments in his films are poignant and lyrical, not threatening. *Giant*, in spite of its richly observed Texan scene, is overlong and shapeless; and it fails to achieve quite the right performance from James Dean as Jett Rink once he has risen in the world and ceased to be the unhappy, questing rebel, so out of sorts with the Texan 'aristocracy' who patronise him for his inability to adapt to their pretensions. In contrast to the unenclosed spaces of *Giant* and *Shane*, the hermetically sealed-up setting in which Anne Frank and her fellow refugees exist could not be more pointed; all the characters in *The Diary of Anne Frank* are very carefully observed and played.

Anthony Mann (who at one stage acted as an assistant to Preston Sturges) moved on from the direction of Westerns to make some of the larger-scale productions of the 1960s. In *El Cid* (1961) and *The Fall of the Roman Empire* (1963) he reveals a

The Fall of the Roman Empire 1963. Director Anthony Mann
Alec Guinness, James Mason

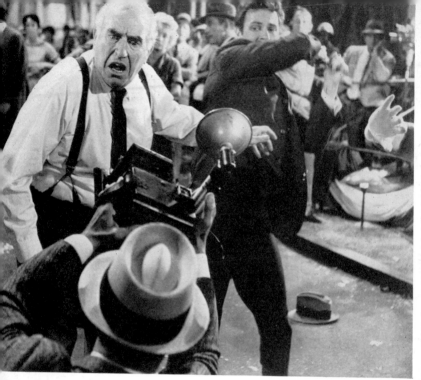

Sweet Bird of Youth 1962. Director Richard Brooks
Ed Begley

far greater response to the character of his locations than to the
characters of people. What matters in *El Cid* is not the flat dialogue
scenes but the Spanish setting—the landscapes and the castle.
It is perhaps a natural enough reaction after working in Westerns,
and Mann excelled in the achievement of magnificent, broad
effects rather than in detail. 'The simpler and more primitive the
story the better . . . I'm interested in drama, and therefore try to
use whatever is effective dramatically . . . It's fascinating to use
masses', are among the points he has expressed in discussing his
work.

Richard Brooks, author, screenwriter and stage director as well
as film-maker, includes among his best-known films *The Blackboard Jungle* (1955), *Cat on a Hot Tin Roof* (1958), *Elmer
Gantry* (1960) and *Sweet Bird of Youth* (1962). *The Blackboard
Jungle*, says Brooks, was the first film 'where I had the chance to
say, no, I don't want to do it except this way'—a right he exercised

when MGM wanted him to put in a scene saying things were, after all, worse in Russia. The actuality of the film, he claimed, derived from what he had himself experienced in his youth. Earlier in his career he had worked on 'story construction' for the documentary type films, *The Killers, Brute Force* and *The Naked City*. More recently, he has made a Western, *The Professionals* (1967). But his principal films operate in the familiar territory of the newer directors, the emotional forcing-house epitomised in the kind of people and the kind of situations to be found in the work of Tennessee Williams. While *Cat on a Hot Tin Roof* had, in 1958, to be toned down, *Sweet Bird of Youth* four years later could be more

The Professionals 1966. Director Richard Brooks
Maria Gomez, Jack Palance

outspoken. It contained a brilliant *tour de force* performance by Geraldine Page as the predatory actress, of whom Brooks has said, 'She may be realistic in her business life, but she is very unrealistic in her personal life. It's a very harsh picture, and I didn't see why the photography had to be as harsh as the content. I thought—here's this harsh picture which has to do with hashish, with castration, bastardy, vicious politics and I don't know what. And I wanted everything to be soft and beautifully coloured. This figure sees everything as soft, and wants it to be that way.'

In *Elmer Gantry* (which ran into censor problems over its last line—'See you in hell, brother') Brooks made, with Burt Lancaster and Jean Simmons, an equally heated exposure of corrupt revivalism, having bought the option on Sinclair Lewis's novel himself. But Brooks, a tough idealist, seems to maintain in his films that good might just conceivably triumph over evil. Of *Elmer Gantry* Brooks has said: 'What I'm trying to say is that revivalism can corrupt and mislead . . . But I want the audience to like Gantry himself, although he's loud and cruel and exhibitionist and blatant. He likes the things of life that we all like . . . Religion used as an ambitious device is contrasted with religion as a cathartic influence, as Sharon experiences it. But Gantry had to leave religion and go back to life.'

Opposite: **Elmer Gantry** 1960. Director Richard Brooks
Burt Lancaster, Jean Simmons

Anatomy of a Murder 1959. Director Otto Preminger
James Stewart, Ben Gazzara

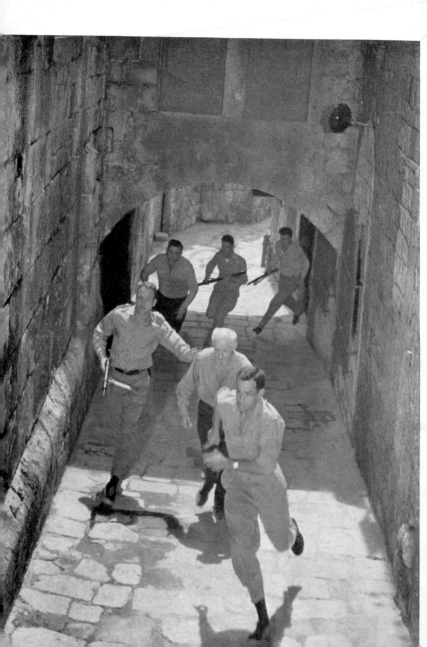

Otto Preminger, who was born in Austria (he is an LL.D of Vienna University) reached the United States in 1936 around the age of 30; he has had considerable experience as actor and director in the theatre. As an established film-maker, he has alternated the wilder shores of realism (*The Man with the Golden Arm*, 1956; *Anatomy of a Murder*, 1959) with essays in the 'larger' subjects (*Exodus*, 1960; *Advise and Consent*, 1962; *The Cardinal*, 1963), and even directed musicals (*Carmen Jones*, 1955, and *Porgy and Bess*, 1958). Otto Preminger has been largely an independent producer–director since the 1950s, and is essentially an actor's director; practically all his films are notable for the performances he brings to the screen (Frank Sinatra in *The Man with the Golden Arm*, Dorothy Dandridge in *Carmen Jones*, Lee Remick in *Anatomy of a Murder*, and Charles Laughton in *Advise and Consent*). Otto Preminger has a showman's *panache*, and knows how to roadshow his films, as well as give an effective performance himself as a prominent world figure. He seems at his best in the realist films, such as *Advise and Consent*, which is the most impressive of his later productions, which include *Bunny Lake is Missing* (1965) and *Hurry Sundown* (1967).

Advise and Consent 1962. Director Otto Preminger
Charles Laughton

Inherit the Wind 1960. Director Stanley Kramer
Spencer Tracy, Fredric March

Stanley Kramer, who began work in films as an editor and scriptwriter during the 1930s, became a producer (for example, of *The Men*, *High Noon*, *Champion* and *The Wild One*) as well as producer–director of such 'social' films as *The Defiant Ones* (1958, on racial antipathies), *On the Beach* (1959, the world after nuclear war), *Inherit the Wind* (1960), which dramatised the so-called 'Monkey Trial' concerned with the persecution of a small-town schoolteacher for teaching Darwinism, and *Judgment at Nuremberg* (1961), the study of a trial in post-war Germany of certain men charged with genocide. One understands what Kramer means when he claims, 'I am a dealer in impact'.

The Hustler 1961. Director Robert Rossen
Paul Newman

But most of the newer directors avoided these wider social issues, preferring subjects which turned on human relationships. Robert Rossen, who had completed *All the King's Men* in 1949, directed *The Hustler* (1961, with Paul Newman), a film about a gambler in a community intent on living entirely by gambling ; as Rossen has put it himself, 'the element common to many of my films is the desire for success, ambition, which is an important element in American life'. Rossen then went on to direct *Lilith* (1964), which is arguably his best, certainly his most sensitive film—an extraordinary, oblique study of human relationships inside a mental hospital, with Warren Beatty, Jean Seberg and Kim Hunter.

Daniel Mann, who belongs roughly to the same age-group as Rossen, was for a while associated with the Actors' Studio in New York in their work for television. In the theatre he directed William Inge's play, *Come Back, Little Sheba*, which was later, in 1952 to become his first film. This pitiful story of two people (finely played by Burt Lancaster and Shirley Booth) who are victims of a forced marriage, was humane, richly theatrical and sentimental; the film was largely an actors' picture. Daniel Mann followed it with Tennessee Williams's *The Rose Tattoo* (1955), which introduced Anna Magnani to Hollywood; *I'll Cry Tomorrow* (1955), a

The Rose Tattoo 1955. Director Daniel Mann
Burt Lancaster, Anna Magnani

Kiss Me Deadly 1955. Director Robert Aldrich
Gaby Rogers

study of recovery from alcoholism featuring Susan Haywood as the singer, Lillian Roth; and later *Butterfield 8* (1960), with a very effective performance from Elizabeth Taylor as a small-town courtesan. Other directors dealt with similarly sensational subjects Laslo Benedek, for example, who came from Europe to the United States in 1937, exposed the pretentiousness of fatherhood in his stylised film version of Arthur Miller's play, *Death of a Salesman* (1951), and of the younger generation in *The Wild One* (1954, with Marlon Brando), a film which set the censor on edge when it reached Britain. Robert Aldrich followed his stylised adaptation from Mickey Spillane, *Kiss Me Deadly* (1955), his melodramatic adaptation of Clifford Odets' play *The Big Knife* (1955, with Rod Steiger and Jack Palance) and *Attack !* (1956, with Eddie Albert

On page 88/89
The Flight of the Phoenix 1965. Director Robert Aldrich
Dan Duryea, James Stewart, Richard Attenborough

Death of a Salesman 1951. Director Laslo Benedek
Fredric March

as a coward in command of an American infantry company) with *The Garment Jungle* (1956), a thriller (credited to Vincent Sherman) exposing union violence and racketeering. His descent into the horror-market with *Whatever Happened to Baby Jane?* (1963) passed the bounds of reasonable credulity, but *The Flight of the Phoenix* (1965) was an uncompromisingly realistic study of survival after a civilian plane crash in a desert. Martin Ritt, a former actor and stage director who has links with the Actors' Studio and considerable experience with television,

Opposite:
The Big Knife 1955. Director Robert Aldrich
Rod Steiger, Jack Palance

The Garment Jungle 1956. Directors Robert Aldrich, Vincent Sherman
Gia Scala

A Man is Ten Feet Tall (Edge of the City) 1956. Director Martin Ritt
John Cassavetes, Sidney Poitier, Kathleen Maguire

established himself in films with *A Man is Ten Feet Tall* (1956; also called *Edge of the City*), in which a wise and humane coloured man, played by Sidney Poitier, is sacrificed to a weak and indifferent white man. Later Ritt was to make a sophisticated Western, *Hud* (1962), with Paul Newman as the amoral son of an old-time Texan cattleman, and, also with Paul Newman, *Cool Hand Luke* (1967).

Cool Hand Luke 1967. Director Stuart Rosenberg
Paul Newman

Among the contemporaries of the newer directors were some with a more unusual and, at times, eccentric talent to draw upon. Preston Sturges, dramatist and screenwriter, was the oldest of these; he was born in 1898, and died at a comparatively early age in 1959. The final exhibition of his particular brilliance came immediately after the war (during which he had made in a single year, 1944, *The Miracle of Morgan's Creek* and *Hail the Conquering Hero*), with two films: *Unfaithfully Yours* (1948) and *The Beautiful Blonde from Bashful Bend* (1949, with Betty Grable). Of these, *Unfaithfully Yours* was the more original and characteristic, with Rex Harrison as a world-famous conductor driven berserk through suspicion of his wife; as he conducts Rossini, Wagner and Tchaikovsky his vision of vengeance works up to a climax he is unable to fulfil when faced by his wholly innocent wife. Sturges, said to have been the inventor of the

Hail the Conquering Hero 1944. Director Preston Sturges
Eddie Bracken

first kiss-proof lipstick (his mother was a cosmetician), was also determined to prove his films free from any traces of conformity. *The Miracle of Morgan's Creek* represents for its period an incredible sleight-of-hand with the censorship; it concerns a girl who has forgotten the identity of the man whom she casually married overnight and by whom she is now pregnant. *Hail the Conquering Hero* delivered a piquant slap at the more stupid aspects of American wartime hero-worship. Both these films (his best) featured Eddie Bracken in a state of distraction. Sturges's best films follow their own seemingly inconsequential way, glorying in their wild improbability, and anyone who wants to derive some moral from them needs to have his own morals examined. These elaborately contrary comedies remain uniquely funny, stripping society of every pet pretension. It is a pity that Sturges's post-war films never matched them in quality.

Unfaithfully Yours 1948. Director Preston Sturges
Rex Harrison

John Huston (described recently in an English woman's magazine as 'last of the great buccaneers') is the son of the late Walter Huston, one of the screen's most vigorous character actors. Huston had been a champion boxer at 18, an actor, a journalist (like his mother), a horseman in the Mexican cavalry—all before he was invited by Sam Goldwyn to become a screenwriter. When this failed, he travelled to Britain (where he kept himself by busking), and then went to Paris, where he studied art and lived by selling sketches. When he returned to the States, he became editor of an illustrated weekly, and later resumed screenwriting. His early scripts included *Juarez* and *Sergeant York*. Then, in 1941, he directed his own adaptation of Dashiel Hammett's *The Maltese Falcon*. Huston's peripatetic career proved an excellent training for the kind of films he was eventually to make. After work in wartime documentary, his later career began with his Mexican location film, *The Treasure of Sierra Madre* (1948), which won two Oscars, for script and direction. The American-made films which followed included *The Asphalt Jungle* (1950)

Opposite:
The Treasure of Sierra Madre 1948. Director John Huston
Walter Huston

The Asphalt Jungle 1950. Director John Huston
Sam Jaffe, Louis Calhern

in which Marilyn Monroe first made her name, and *The Red Badge of Courage* (1951; the subject of Lillian Ross's celebrated study of Hollywood's methods, *Picture*). After this he made a series of films which were British (*The African Queen*, shot in Africa; *Moby Dick*, with locations in Madeira). Since 1952 his permanent home has been in Ireland. He is now, like his ancestors, an Irish citizen.

The Red Badge of Courage 1951. Director John Huston
Audie Murphy

Freud (The Secret Passion) 1962. Director John Huston
Montgomery Clift, Susannah York

In a sense, Huston's work is an extension of his life and interests. His films have no common root except that they express something he enjoys doing, ranging from sophisticated farce (*Beat the Devil*) to *The Bible* (though he describes himself as a 'philosophical atheist') or *Freud* (*The Secret Passion*, 1962, with Montgomery Clift), which is surely one of his best films; 'We had to make the script starkly simple because the ideas are so complex,' he said. He developed Freud's pursuit of his patients' neuroses in the form of a psychological thriller. But he remains essentially a director of action—the round-up of the mustang in *The Misfits* (1960) shows this—and his capacity for sympathetic observation of human behaviour, however odd, is his strength. There is more than a touch of melancholy in most of his work which comes, perhaps, from recollections of rootlessness in his youth.

The Misfits 1960. Director John Huston
Marilyn Monroe, Clark Gable

Macbeth 1948. Director Orson Welles
Orson Welles

Another more or less expatriate director is Orson Welles, whose immediate post-war productions were made in America (*The Stranger*, 1946; *The Lady from Shanghai*, 1947; *Macbeth*, shot in 23 days in 1948). His later films are credited to Morocco (*Othello*, 1951), Spain (*Mr Arcadin*, 1955 and *Chimes at Midnight*, 1965) and France–Italy–West Germany (*The Trial*, 1962). Only *Touch of Evil* (1958) is American. Since 1946 he has also acted in over thirty films, including his own, and directed many stage productions.

Welles is one of those rare, instinctive directors whose first film (*Citizen Kane*, 1941) was a masterpiece because he applied the whole of his great talent to concentrated study of the medium before he made it. 'John Ford was my movie teacher,' he said in an interview with Dilys Powell. 'My own style has nothing to do with his, but *Stagecoach* was my movie text-book.' He brought to the cinema his outstanding experience in theatre and sound radio and an innovating approach to dramatic presentation second only to that of Kazan in the United States. He was still only 25 when he made *Citizen Kane* with members of his theatre company, the Mercury Players, which he formed in 1938. It was his resounding success and originality which gave him the unique opportunity to do what he liked in his first film, but it caused such a *furore* and did so badly at the box-office that he forfeited all further right to the freedom of the screen.

Since this time he has mostly wandered from place to place in Europe, realising now and then one of the projects of his fertile imagination and making magnificent, *tour de force* appearances in other peoples' films. The problem for him has always been that he seems unable to adjust his copious capacities to the strait-jacket of commercial film-making, which alone can provide him with the resources he needs. When, on occasion, he manages to piece these resources together, he tends to make films which only partially realise his full intentions, and he often sacrifices clarity of story-line to highly developed atmosphere. His later Hollywood film, *Touch of Evil* (an improvement on his moral thrillers of 1946–47), shows how corruption can become contagious during an investigation following the murder of a millionaire on the US-Mexican border. Welles's frequent concern with moral issues, with justice and injustice, receives clearer treatment in this film. It is one of his best, having great virtuosity of technique, including long takes and magnificently-conceived visual effects achieved through extremes of light and shadow. After all, he has said, 'I like the camera—no, that's too mild a word. I love it.'

On pages 104/105
From Here to Eternity 1953. Director Fred Zinnemann
Montgomery Clift

Opposite:
Touch of Evil 1958. Director Orson Welles
Orson Welles

With Nicholas Ray, Fred Zinnemann and Robert Wise, we come to the directors among the newer men whose style in film-making carries us forward to the work of the younger generation. Fred Zinnemann, born in Austria, came to the United States from Europe in 1930. He had made, as we have seen, a number of notable films after the war, including *The Men* and *High Noon* (both mentioned earlier), *Teresa* (1951), *Member of the Wedding* (1952), *From Here to Eternity* (1958) and his narcotics film, *A Hatful of Rain* (1957). He has claimed to have been influenced in America by the new approach to acting led by Orson Welles's Mercury Theatre and the Group Theatre (which later became the Actors' Studio). His later films (including *The Nun's Story*, shot in the Congo, and *The Sundowners*, shot in Australia) seemed heavier, with a strong literary bias which was more tightly controlled in his British film, *A Man for all Seasons* (adapted for the screen by Robert Bolt from his own play).

Robert Wise, whose early career in films included editing *Citizen Kane* and *The Magnificent Ambersons* before directing the realist film *The Set-up* in 1949, has in his maturity made films of widely differing kinds. He has mixed *The Day the Earth Stood Still* (1951), one of the best of the early science-fiction films, and the violent, sentimental film, *Somebody up there Likes Me* (1956; featuring Paul Newman as Rocky Graziano) with, to take his more notable films: *Executive Suite* (1954), a study of politics and palace revolution in a star-ridden boardroom, *I Want to Live* (1959), with Susan Hayward as a woman facing the electric chair, and *Two for the Seesaw* (1962), a beautifully played study of a passing relationship between a dancing instructress (Shirley MacLaine) and a married man (Robert Mitchum) estranged from a wife he still, in fact, loves and to whom he finally returns. He directed *West Side Story* (1961), the musical by Arthur Laurents and Leonard Bernstein, in close association with the choreographer, Jerome Robbins; in spite of its sentimental link with *Romeo and Juliet*, the film is visually impressive, and was to a considerable extent shot on location in New York. Wise was later to direct a far more conventional musical, *The Sound of Music* (1964) and the war film, *The Sand Pebbles* (1967).

Opposite:
I Want to Live 1959. Director Robert Wise
Susan Hayward

Nicholas Ray had worked initially in the theatre with John Houseman, and he was Kazan's assistant in Hollywood on *A Tree Grows in Brooklyn*. His first film, *They Live by Night* (1947), belonged to the documentary realist movement; some of his later films were to be spectacles—*King of Kings* (1961) and

Opposite:
Two for the Seesaw 1962. Director Robert Wise
Shirley MacLaine, Robert Mitchum

West Side Story 1961. Directed by Robert Wise, Jerome Robbins
Richard Beymer, George Chakiris

55 Days at Peking (1962). But with *Rebel Without a Cause* (1955, and starring, of course, James Dean) he made his most influential film. This was, in part at least, improvised with Dean. It became, of the three star parts this young actor played in little more than a single year before his death in 1955, the one which did most to create the Dean 'image'—that of the misunderstood adolescent whose frustrated need for affection leads him to behave in a way that both mystifies and scandalises the elder generation. Dean's death in his Porsche on the way to Salinas seemed like an act of self-immolation, a symbolic martyrdom. When Joan Collins published what she claimed were his messages from the world of the spirits, half a million copies were sold, while the ruined car became the source for 'relics' sold at fancy prices. *Rebel Without a Cause* heralded an altogether deeper degree of identification between the star and his public, while the subjects in which such stars appeared drew closer to the experiences and needs at least of the younger generation in the audience, to whom the American cinema of the later 1950s and 1960s seemed to be specially addressed.

The new stars, like the new films, were more challenging, more disturbing than the old. They approached their work with a quality of concentration which stripped the mask off the established, recognisable, *genre* performance, substituting a kind of naked personality for those former masterpieces of starmanship. Audiences began to find themselves unaccountably involved with these new personalities precisely because they seemed to be people on the screen, not players. Lee Strasberg, an American stage director born in Austria who had been producing plays in the United States since 1925, founded the Group Theatre and later in 1948 the Actors' Studio in New York for the purpose of enabling established but dedicated actors and actresses to broaden and deepen the range of their performances ; it is well-known that the so-called 'method' acting associated with Strasberg was to some extent derived from Stanislavsky's principles of training for the Moscow Art Theatre at the turn of the century—'The appearance of the Moscow Art Theatre and of Duse electrified us,' wrote Strasberg. 'On the one hand a superb ensemble able to fill each moment of a play with life, each actor concerned not with the importance or unimportance of his part, but with his relation to the scene, to other characters, each moment played with full conviction and reality. On the other, an actress who remained always herself, yet always changed.' Strasberg's Studio was to become something of a myth, but it meant in effect that players of innate quality learnt by trial and error how to involve themselves more completely, more emotionally with the characters they assumed so that they seemed to become very closely identified with them. Strasberg has described his 'method' quite simply : 'The chief aim of the Studio's method is to allow the actor to get right down to his emotions and then to express emotions fully on the stage. It seeks to free him from all hindrances to the full exploiting of his talents.' At its best, a 'method' performance by such actors and actresses as Marlon Brando, James Dean, Eli Wallach, Paul Newman, Montgomery Clift, Julie Harris, Eva Marie Saint, Shelley Winters, Kim Hunter, Marilyn Monroe or June Havoc brought an altogether new quality of depth, of inner realisation of psychological detail to the screen; they played characters whose natures, often ambiguous, required genuine penetration by actor and audience alike, in much the same way as people have to be understood by a process of observation in real life.

Rebel Without a Cause 1955. Director Nicholas Ray
James Dean, Jim Backus, Ann Doran

The work of the Actors' Studio was particularly associated with Elia Kazan, a Turkish-born American who had worked with Strasberg in the Group Theatre, and achieved success both as actor and director; and also with the American dramatist Tennessee Williams. Williams made his name initially as a dramatist on Broadway in 1945 with *The Glass Menagerie*, the first of a long succession of plays which offer strongly developed parts for both actors and actresses. These were plays in which the 'method' approach to performance was peculiarly effective.

It was Kazan who transferred this new, intense form of acting to the American screen. His earliest films, as we have seen, were a part of the realist movement; but from *The Glass Menagerie* (1950) and in particular, *A Streetcar Named Desire* (also 1950) onwards, his films (by no means always successful at the box-office) set

Opposite:
A Streetcar Named Desire 1950. Director Elia Kazan
Marlon Brando, Kim Hunter

The Glass Menagerie 1950. Director Elia Kazan
Jane Wyman, Arthur Kennedy

Viva Zapata! 1951. Director Elia Kazan
Marlon Brando

On the Waterfront 1954. Director Elia Kazan
Marlon Brando

standards of 'performance in depth' and of technical achievement
in sustaining atmosphere and psychological tension which gave a
lead to the more advanced American cinema. The remaining
principal films of this second period include: *Viva Zapata !* (1951,
with an intense, rather declamatory script by John Steinbeck), in
which Marlon Brando plays the Mexican peasant rebel leader
against the regime of the dictator Diaz; *On the Waterfront* (1954),
with Brando playing a young dock worker whose dawning con-
science leads him to oppose single-handed the powerful union
boss who 'protects' the dockers; *East of Eden* (1954; the first
effective demonstration of how widescreen could be used for an
intimate subject), in which James Dean plays the inarticulate son
of a father incapable of understanding his need for maternal

East of Eden 1954. Director Elia Kazan
James Dean, Raymond Massey

A Face in the Crowd 1956. Director Elia Kazan
Andy Griffith, Patricia Neal

Splendour in the Grass 1960. Director Elia Kazan
Warren Beatty, Pat Hingle

affection; *Baby Doll* (1956), a study of sexual obsession in a decadent Southern household; *A Face in the Crowd* (1957), in which a crude television 'personality' exploits and is exploited by the politicians; *Splendour in the Grass* (1960), in which an adolescent girl, played by Natalie Wood, is driven to suicide through the misplaced solicitude of her parents; and *The Anatolian Smile* (*America, America*, 1963), which is concerned with emigration to America and was shot in Turkey and Greece. In all of his films, Kazan absorbs himself in the nature of his chosen actors and gives them their heads to develop under the camera in large and demanding parts. 'He will find out what makes you tick, how you operate, how you live,' Karl Malden has said; 'and he in turn will adjust to you.' Kazan is, above everything else, an actors' director, either discovering or developing the latent talents of such stars as Brando, Dean, Warren Beatty (brother of Shirley Mac-Laine), Malden, Kim Hunter, Eva Marie Saint, Carroll Baker, Lee Remick and Natalie Wood.

Shadows 1960. Director John Cassavetes
Lelia Goldoni, Ben Carruthers

In an interview with Robin Bean in 1962, Kazan discussed his attitude to his players: 'In a film you can photograph a person thinking, you can photograph thought; the camera can also be used as a microscope, it is a penetrating device by which you can photograph the inner experience of a person, particularly a sensitive person. Things that wouldn't count on stage are most precious in film. The essential job is to get the truth of the experience going on in the actor; if he will really experience what's happening truthfully then it's worth photographing. I am trying in all the films I do either to eliminate as much dialogue as I can or to make it an embroidery on the outskirts of the action. Part of the behaviour *is* what they say, but not the essential part of it, and in that sense I think my work is getting more cinematic.' He has, as one might expect, an equally strong feeling for writers as for actors: 'I try to *realise* the author,' he has said, in the French sense of the word *réalisation*. Writing about Budd Schulberg's *A Face in the Crowd*, an exposure of the ease with which a brash, conscienceless television personality can corrupt both himself and the society he 'entertains', Kazan said: 'There can't be a fine picture without a fine script. There can't be a fine script without a first-class writer. A first-class writer won't do a first-class work unless he feels the picture is *his*.' More than anyone in the 1950s, Kazan brought a theatre director's real respect for the writer into American film-making, and in the process did much to overcome the inhibiting restrictions of the Hollywood censor code as it was formerly applied.

Another actor of stage and television who developed his own method of evolving acting on the screen was John Cassavetes. Over a prolonged period he finally completed *Shadows* (1960) with the voluntary help of a cast of players from his theatre workshop in New York. The actors themselves formulated the story-line, which is about a girl seduced by a white boy who does not at the time realise she belongs to a coloured family. Cassavetes has written in *Films and Filming*: 'With *Shadows* we tried something completely different, in that we not only improvised in terms of the words, but we improvised in terms of motions. So the cameraman also improvised; he had to follow the artists and light generally, so that the actor could move when and wherever he pleased. A strange and interesting thing happened, in that the

Louisiana Story 1948. Director Robert Flaherty

camera, in following the people, followed them smoothly and beautifully, simply because people have a natural rhythm. Whereas when they rehearse something according to a technical mark, they begin to be jerky and unnatural, and no matter how talented they are, the camera has a difficult time in following them.' Cassavetes was in effect re-discovering the technique of camera-observation originally developed by Robert Flaherty, who completed his last, beautiful film, *Louisiana Story*, in 1948 among the Cajun people living in the bayou country of Louisiana. Though in the case of Cassavetes the result was not continuously effective (the actors at times visibly losing their complete hold on character and situation), the experiment proved in the best scenes (between the girl and her lover) that such improvised acting could be authentic and touching. Cassavetes's later films, *Too Late Blues* (1961) and *A Child is Waiting* (1962), were more conventional in subject and treatment, though they contained effective acting.

In the movement towards independence, many actors have become their own producers. Among them are Brando, Burt Lancaster, Kirk Douglas, Richard Widmark and, in his own way, Orson Welles. Actors may or may not be shrewd in choosing the characters in which they present themselves on the screen. Brando's initial choice was *One-Eyed Jacks* (1960). Set in the 1880s, the story features Rio, a young ex-convict obsessed by the need to avenge himself on his betrayer, a former accomplice who is now a sheriff and whose step-daughter he seduces. The film is self-indulgent, brooding and full of curious, dark psychological undertones, which contrast with the romantic seacoast settings of Monterey. Burt Lancaster's choice as a producer, or co-producer, of films in which he also starred has perhaps been more justified ; they include *Apache*, *The Sweet Smell of Success* (directed by Alexander Mackendrick from Britain), and *Birdman of Alcatraz*, the true story of a convict who established his own aviary in his prison cell and became a noted authority on birds. Other films promoted or directed by actors include : *The Night of the Hunter* (1955) directed by Charles Laughton, Karl Malden's *Time Limit !* (1957), which he directed, Richard Widmark's production of *The Secret Ways* (1961), John Wayne's production of *The Alamo* (1960), which he also directed, and Warren Beatty's production of *Bonnie and Clyde* (1967).

The Connection 1960. Director Shirley Clarke

The experimenters

In conscious revolt against all forms of conventional cinema in the
United States has been the large-scale development of 'underground' and avant-garde films, especially in New York. These
productions represent the challenge of non-conformity to the
Hollywood 'establishment', and the film-makers themselves are
linked to the various manifestations of revolt fashionable in
American society. This is the cinema which, at its most ambitious,
has produced such films as Lionel Rogosin's *On the Bowery*
(1954) and *Come Back, Africa* (1958), *Guns of the Trees* (Jonas
Mekas, 1962), *The Connection* (Shirley Clarke, 1960), *Pull my
Daisy* (Robert Frank and Alfred Leslie, 1959), Joseph Strick's
The Savage Eye (1959, with Ben Maddow and Sidney Meyers)
and *The Balcony* (1963), *Hallelujah the Hills* (Adolfas Mekas,
1963) and Frank Perry's *David and Lisa* (1962). Strick's most
striking and successful production has been *Ulysses*, made in
Ireland during 1966. This has been distributed in many countries
in a form which represented an outright challenge to censorship.

Whether or not America's extreme underground cinema will have
any effective influence on American above-ground film-making
has yet to be seen. Lionel Rogosin formed his New American
Cinema Group in New York during 1960, and in their initial
manifesto proclaimed: 'The official Cinema all over the world is
running out of breath. It is morally corrupt, aesthetically obsolete,
thematically superficial, temperamentally boring.' These film-
makers feel that the old prohibitions are receding far too slowly

The Balcony 1963. Director Joseph Strick

Hallelujah the Hills 1963. Director Adolfas Mekas

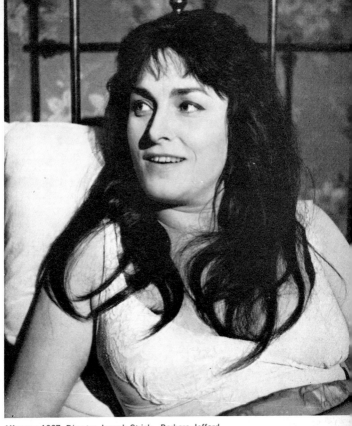

Ulysses 1967. Director Joseph Strick Barbara Jefford

and that the old pressure groups, such as the former Legion of Decency (the Catholic censorship front now renamed the National Catholic Center for Motion Pictures), are still far too inhibiting. The underground movies of New York are often shown on a hit-and-run basis in small club cinemas, and sometimes present films which attempt to parallel in visual action the printed words of Miller and Burroughs. Film-makers such as Kenneth Anger (*Fireworks*, a study of homosexuality, and *Scorpio Rising*), Curtis Harrington (who made the feature *Night Tide* in 1961 after a series of experimental films), Jack Smith (*Flaming Creatures*, a film about a group of transvestites) and Peter Emanuel Goldman (*Echoes of Silence*, 1963, 'a diary made with a camera instead of a pen'), are leading exponents of a new cinema in which anything, even boredom, is given direct expression on the screen.

The musical

The musical is a form of film-making with, in general, its own specialised directors. During the 1930s American screen musicals had to free themselves from the structure and choreography of the stage shows from which they were derived, creating a new, free-flowing continuity in which the song-and-dance 'numbers' and 'routines' became fully integrated with the action and, above all, with the mood and fantasy of the film. This was finally achieved, after the example set initially by Mamoulian, Lubitsch and Berkeley, in the easy-going, intimate productions featuring Fred Astaire and Ginger Rogers—starting with *The Gay Divorce* (1934). Musicals then entered a new phase with Vincente Minnelli's *Meet me in St Louis* (1944, with Judy Garland), while the later work of the key directors of musicals from the 1930s—George Sidney (*Anchors Aweigh*, 1945; *Annie Get Your Gun*, 1950; *Kiss Me Kate*, 1953; *Pal Joey*, 1957) and the former stage producer and pupil of Stanislavky, Rouben Mamoulian (*Summer Holiday*, 1947)—added to the sheer visual virtuosity which was to make the period 1944–54 the summit of American achievement in a form which still remains uniquely characteristic of Hollywood's technical skill and artifice. This includes the period of the direction and screen choreography of Stanley Donen (*On the Town*, 1949,

On The Town 1949. Directors Stanley Donen, Gene Kelly
Vera Ellen

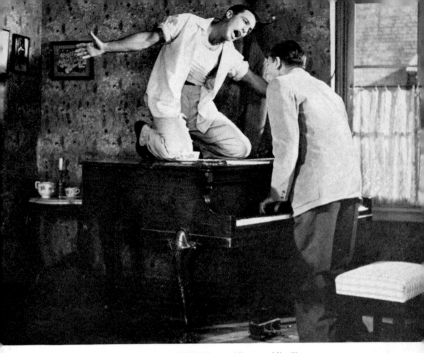

An American in Paris 1950. Director Vincente Minelli
Gene Kelly

and *Singin' in the Rain*, 1952, both co-directed with Gene Kelly;
Seven Brides for Seven Brothers, 1954; *Funny Face,* 1950; *The
Pajama Game,* 1957, co-directed with George Abbott), Charles
Walters, director of dance sequences in so many films, and of
Minnelli's further work (*The Pirate,* 1947; *An American in Paris,*
1950; *The Bandwagon,* 1953). (Minnelli, like Donen, directs
'straight' films, such as *Father of the Bride,* 1950.) Other, non-
specialist, directors contributed films which maintained a high
standard—Cukor's re-make of *A Star is Born* (1954, with Judy
Garland) and *My Fair Lady* (1964), and Mankiewicz's *Guys and
Dolls* (1955). If anything led to the decline of technical virtuosity
and imagination in the direction of the musical it was its inevitable
association with the larger screens of the mid-1950s. Musicals
became, once more, spectacles enlarging but seldom liberating the
big-scale stage productions from which they came, such as
South Pacific and *The Sound of Music.*

Father of the Bride 1950. Director Vincente Minnelli
Spencer Tracy, Joan Bennett

There's No Business Like Show Business 1954. Director Walter Lang
Marilyn Monroe

The new generation

If there is any common characteristic to unite the directors whose work belongs most closely to the contemporary American cinema, it is the fact that many of them share experience in television direction. A number of them, too, write their own scripts. The work of some shows a particular kind of stylishness which marks them off from the older directors, though not all of them are necessarily very young men. To take directors whose reputations have been achieved during the late 1950s and the 1960s: Frank Tashlin was around 50 when he made *The Man from the Diners' Club* (1963), Blake Edwards around 40 at the time of *The Pink Panther* (also 1963), Richard Quine around 33 at the time of *Paris When it Sizzles* (1963), Sidney Lumet around 33 at the time of *Twelve Angry Men* (1957), John Frankenheimer around 30 at the time of *Birdman of Alcatraz* and *The Manchurian Candidate* in 1962 and Roger Corman also round 30 when his prolific output of horror films started round 1955. Tashlin had the most unusual start—as an animator working for Disney. Tashlin, like Edwards, Quine and Corman, was a screenwriter before taking up direction. Edwards, Lumet, Franklin Schaffner and Frankenheimer (who had, like Quine, been an actor) have all worked for television.

Twelve Angry Men 1957. Director Sidney Lumet
Henry Fonda

The stylishness of certain of these directors is evident not only in the highly polished surface they give to their films—elegance and edge in the dialogue, gaiety and inconsequence when working in comedy—but also in the unconventional twists they give to stories which are still basically box-office. Tashlin's comedy can seem painstaking, but he has his own individual, elaborate sense of humour. His films include: *Will Success Spoil Rock Hunter?* (1957), the sentimental *Cinderfella* (1960) and *Disorderly Orderly* (1964), both with Jerry Lewis; *Bachelor Flat* (1961, with Terry-Thomas); *The Man from the Diner's Club* (1963), in which the unique charm of Danny Kaye is exploited in the part of a nervous clerk entangled with a gangster, and *Caprice* (1967). (Kaye, whose charm seems so inconsequent but is in fact very

Bachelor Flat 1961. Director Frank Tashlin
Terry-Thomas, Richard Beymer

The Man from the Diner's Club 1963. Director Frank Tashlin
Cara Williams

professional and assured, has appeared in films, often indifferent in quality, during the post-war period; one of his best was *The Secret Life of Walter Mitty* as early as 1947.) Richard Quine, another director primarily of comedy, broke into direction through screenwriting during the early 1950s. His earlier comedies included *Operation Mad Ball* (1957), a satirical farce at the expense of the army, and *It Happened to Jane* (1959), both with Jack Lemmon and Ernie Kovacs. Among his later films are *Paris When it Sizzles* (1963), which had a guest appearance by Noel Coward, and

Opposite:
Paris When it Sizzles 1963. Director Richard Quine
Noel Coward

The Secret Life of Walter Mitty 1947. Director Norman Z. McLeod
Danny Kaye, Boris Karloff

How to Murder Your Wife (1964). Blake Edwards's most interesting films include *Breakfast at Tiffany's* (1961, with Audrey Hepburn as the maddeningly engaging Holly Golightly), *Days of Wine and Roses* (1962, with Jack Lemmon and Lee Remick, an oversentimental study of alcoholism among the public relations set), and *The Pink Panther* (1963, with Peter Sellers as an incompetent detective).

Opposite:
Breakfast at Tiffany's 1961. Director Blake Edwards
Audrey Hepburn

The Pink Panther 1963. Director Blake Edwards
David Niven, Robert Wagner

Delbert Mann's best-known films show very clearly the influence of his work for stage and television. *Marty* (1955), which won him a director's Oscar, and *Bachelor Party* (1957) show very ordinary people at important moments in their lives; in *Marty*, a man and a woman who, when they eventually fall in love at a time when their youth is behind them, discover they are not such unattractive 'dogs' as they had believed; and, in *Bachelor Party*, another 'ordinary' man and his friends living it up the night before his wedding. Delbert Mann's later films, such as *Middle of the Night* (1959) and *The Dark at the Top of the Stairs* (1960), depend largely for their effect on a similar authenticity of background and characterisation.

Sidney Lumet has spoken about the effect of an initial career in television on his work for the cinema. He experimented with very quick cutting: 'We did a lot of this kind of insane cutting in the early days in television, when often television technique was far in advance of movies . . . We were doing cuts as fast as a finger could move.' This was the technique he was to introduce later

Bachelor Party 1957. Director Delbert Mann
Philip Abbott

in the shock-cuts representing the agonised recollections of the elderly Jew (played by Rod Steiger) in *The Pawnbroker* (1963). In an interview with Robin Bean, Lumet reveals another important asset of the television director—what he calls 'the emotional meaning of the lenses'. He said: 'A lens in itself has a certain kind of impact. If one takes, let's say, a close up: the same size head shot on an 18-mm lens has a different emotional feeling than when shot on a 75-mm lens. The opening up of lenses, and focal lengths, is a dramatic tool. This was one tremendous advantage of television—your eye became terribly sensitised to what the lens itself was doing.' Lumet's first film, *Twelve Angry Men* (1957, adapted from Reginald Rose's television play, originally directed by Schaffner) gave spendid opportunities for the actors playing the men enclosed against their will within the four walls of the jury-room. A similar claustrophobia dominates *Long Day's Journey into Night* (1962), with its exact and detailed characterisation by Dean Stockwell, Jason Robards, Katherine Hepburn and Ralph Richardson. Lumet defended this splendid

The Pawnbroker 1963. Director Sidney Lumet
Rod Steiger, Thelma Oliver

The Group 1966. Director Sidney Lumet
Kathleen Widdoes, Joan Hackett, Mary-Robin Redd, Shirley Knight

film from the critics who said it was theatrical and static: 'There was more sheer physical technique in that movie, in its editing and camerawork, than anything you are liable to see for twenty years.' Nor is he afraid of dialogue: 'I am a great believer in words in films, and I think that the idea of literature being dead so far as cinema is concerned is one of those temporary little fads.' He said this in connection with *The Fugitive Kind* (1960), which was based on Tennessee Williams's play, *Orpheus Descending* and starred Joanne Woodward and Marlon Brando. His other films, *Fail Safe* (1963), *The Hill* (1964) and *The Deadly Affair* (1966) —both British films—and *The Group* (1966) depend equally on precise characterisation. *The Group* and *Who's Afraid of Virginia Woolf?* (1966), Mike Nichols's screen adaptation of Edward

On pages 142/143
Who's Afraid of Virginia Woolf? 1966. Director Mike Nichols
Elizabeth Taylor, Richard Burton

Fail Safe 1963. Director Sidney Lume
Henry Fonda

The Manchurian Candidate 1962. Director John Frankenheimer
Frank Sinatra, Laurence Harvey

144

Albee's stageplay featuring Richard Burton and Elizabeth Taylor, together constitute the most considerable challenge so far from within the commercial cinema itself to the gradually receding American screen censorship code.

John Frankenheimer, who worked originally as an assistant to Lumet, has in his more recent films exploited contemporary political subjects with striking technical effect. In *The Manchurian Candidate* (1962) brainwashing is treated with an extravagant, grotesque humour; *Seven Days in May* (1963) shows how the military assume power in the United States; while in *Seconds*

Seconds 1966. Director John Frankenheimer
Rock Hudson, Karl Swenson

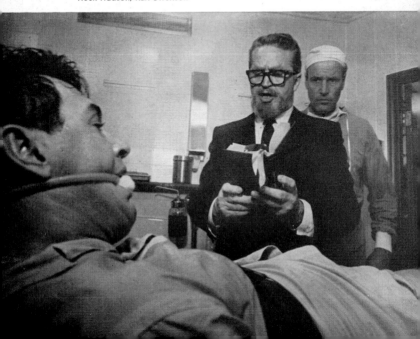

All Fall Down 1962. Director John Frankenheimer
Evans Evans, Brandon de Wilde

The Wild Angels 1966. Director Roger Corman
Peter Fonda

(1966) men are re-modelled in order to undertake a new life. His other films, including *All Fall Down* (1962), the exposure of a small-town family, and *The Young Savages* (1961), though equally impersonal and objective, are less extravagant, more serious. But Frankenheimer's films are mostly thrillers with a skilful psychological or technological twist. Roger Corman, too, after specialising in 'horror' films, has turned more recently to films of psychological violence in *The Wild Angels* (1966) and *The Saint Valentine's Day Massacre* (1967).

The Saint Valentine's Day Massacre 1967. Director Roger Corman

The Best Man 1963. Director Franklin Schaffner
Henry Fonda, Lee Tracy

Franklin Schaffner (who directed Alec Guinness in his first television appearance in the United States) was chosen to direct Gore Vidals's political play, *The Best Man* (1964), which Vidal made into one of the most intelligent scripts the American cinema has had in recent years. *The Best Man* deals with backstage intrigue during a party convention at which a Presidential nominee has to be chosen. The film depended on establishing verisimilitude in both characterisation and background; it succeeded through superb matching of genuine convention coverage and the reconstructed material, together with the authority with which an excellent cast, led by Henry Fonda, played. Schaffner's earlier film, *Woman of Summer* (1963)—adapted from a sentimental play by William Inge about a tarnished beauty-queen (Joanne Woodward) who feels forced to give up an immature lover—though no more than promising, showed his considerable capacity to handle actors. In both cases, he rehearsed his cast fully before they faced the cameras.

Stanley Kubrick was brought up in the Bronx, the son of a doctor who was a keen photographer. Kubrick himself showed a similar flair, and he worked initially as a staff photographer for *Look*. Then he progressed through making documentaries to directing his first feature films, *Fear and Desire* (1953), a study of four soldiers trapped behind enemy lines, and *Killer's Kiss* (1955),

Killer's Kiss 1955. Director Stanley Kubrick
Frank Silvera, Jamie Smith

both of which he made largely on his own initiative with the help of borrowed money. Kubrick wrote his own screenplays and, as few other directors have succeeded in doing, pressured his way into big-time commercial cinema more or less on his own terms. *The Killing* (1956), a crime story in which all the emphasis is on the individual characters of the members of a gang whose leader is played by Stirling Hayden, completed his apprenticeship; there followed *Paths of Glory* (1958, backed jointly by Kirk Douglas and United Artists), a story of military injustice during World War I, *Spartacus* (1960), *Lolita* (1962), *Dr Strangelove, or How I Learned to Stop Worrying and Love the Bomb* (1963) and *2001: a Space Odyssey* (1967). Kubrick, as strong an in-

Dr Strangelove, or How I Learned to Stop Worrying and Love the Bomb 1963. Director Stanley Kubrick
Peter Sellers, George C. Scott, Peter Bull

Paths of Glory 1958. Director Stanley Kubrick
Kirk Douglas, Adolphe Menjou

dividualist as the American cinema possesses, has worked in England since 1962.

Kubrick is less concerned with the mechanics of plot than he is with subject and situation; he has said: 'I think that the best plot is no apparent plot. I like a slow start, the start that gets under the audience's skin and involves them so that they can appreciate grace notes and soft tones and don't have to be pounded over the head with plot points and suspense hooks.' He belongs to that modern movement in film-making, perhaps more European than American, which bases its interests on the real ambivalences of human nature rather than on creating clear-cut characters for the fulfilment of a story-teller's plot. He is still under 40, and he is perhaps the single most original talent among the younger generation of American film-makers.

In comparison with the United States, no country can show an equal range of talent among its film-makers, though the work of certain individual directors, notably in Europe, represents a more remarkable achievement than that of the Americans in exploring and widening the frontiers of the cinema. But in the United States, the oldest generation, led by Ford and Hitchcock, contributes continually to the mainstream of the cinema, alongside the youngest talents, represented by such men as Frankenheimer, Strick, Lumet and Kubrick. In between them the middle generation, including Wilder, Kramer, Huston, Brooks, Mankiewicz and Ritt, keep up a powerful flow of work. Only Kazan seemed, during the 1960s, to have deserted the cinema—temporarily, we must hope.

There are few countries in the world which are completely out of touch with the American cinema, even though some of the less developed do not always see it at its best, while others, for political reasons, may be deprived of it altogether. Nevertheless, a tremendous power lies in the hands of those who take the lead in American film-making, and with the breaking down of the traditional moulds of entertainment, the opportunities before them are all the greater.

Festival 1967. Director Murray Lerner
Joan Baez

On pages 154/155
The Happening 1967. Director Elliot Silverstein
Anthony Quinn, Martha Hyer

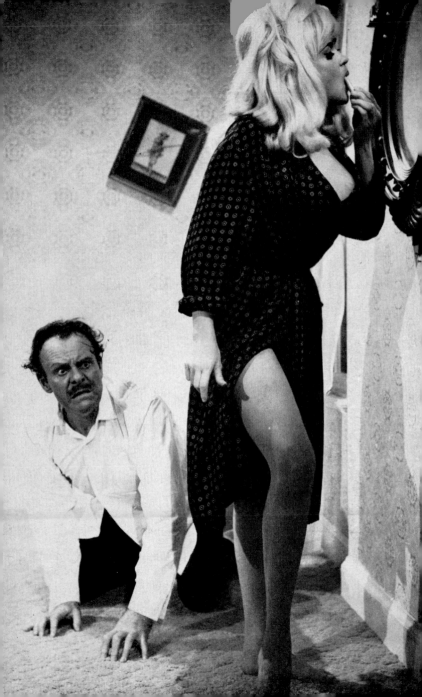

Opposite:
A Guide for the Married Man 1967. Director Gene Kelly
Terry-Thomas, Jayne Mansfield

Divorce American Style 1967. Director Bud Yorkin
Dick van Dyke, Debbie Reynolds

Bonnie and Clyde 1967. Director Arthur Penn
Warren Beatty, Faye Dunaway

Index